Tasting
THE CAPE

Tasting
THE CAPE

GUIDE TO THE
CAPE
Winelands

Jean-Pierre Rossouw

PENGUIN BOOKS

PENGUIN BOOKS

Published by the Penguin Group
Penguin Books (South Africa) (Pty) Ltd, 24 Sturdee Avenue, Rosebank, Johannesburg 2196, South Africa
Penguin Group (USA) Inc, 375 Hudson Street, New York, New York 10014, USA
Penguin Group (Canada), 90 Eglinton Avenue East, Suite 700, Toronto, Ontario, Canada M4P 2Y3 (a division of Pearson Penguin Canada Inc)
Penguin Books Ltd, 80 Strand, London WC2R 0RL, England
Penguin Ireland, 25 St Stephen's Green, Dublin 2, Ireland (a division of Penguin Books Ltd)
Penguin Group (Australia), 250 Camberwell Road, Camberwell, Victoria 3124, Australia (a division of Pearson Australia Group Pty Ltd)
Penguin Books India Pvt Ltd, 11 Community Centre, Panchsheel Park, New Delhi – 110 017, India
Penguin Group (NZ), 67 Apollo Drive, Mairangi Bay, Auckland 1310, New Zealand (a division of Pearson New Zealand Ltd)

Penguin Books (South Africa) (Pty) Ltd, Registered Offices:
24 Sturdee Avenue, Rosebank, Johannesburg 2196, South Africa

www.penguinbooks.co.za

First published as *Mixed Case – A Unique Guide to the Cape Winelands* in 2004 by Struik Publishers (a division of New Holland Publishing (South Africa) (Pty) Ltd)
This edition published by Penguin Books (South Africa) (Pty) Ltd 2010

Text copyright © Jean-Pierre Rossouw 2010
Maps copyright © Struik 2004

All rights reserved
The moral right of the author has been asserted

ISBN 9780143026334

Typeset by Nix Design in 11/14 pt Bulmer BT
Cover: mr design
Printed and bound by UltraLitho, Johannesburg

Disclaimer
While every effort has been made to ensure accuracy, the author and publisher will not be liable for any inconvenience or loss resulting from possible inaccuracies. Information such as telephne numbers, email addresses, roads and maps may have changed since the author researched them and the publisher would appreciate updated information.

Once you've drunk a wine, its story is not yet complete. If it has a strong personality it lingers in memory forever, or else it's an instant snapshot of that moment in time – the place and the people. And a great deal has come before: a line that can be traced back through the human interpreters and into the grape and then the soil and then the multiple unnameable elements that we simply call weather.

So, here's to the eternity contained in every bottle and all the friends and family with whom I've shared this liquid time.

Contents

INTRODUCTION

THE CHARACTERS

The Western Cape Wine Regions

Key

Grandes Dames	G
Big Hitters	B
Corporates	C
Futurists	F
Individualists	I
Stylists	S
Democrats	D
Other Notable Farms	🍷

Constantia region

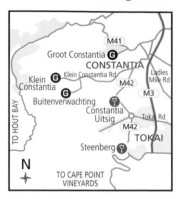

Durbanville region

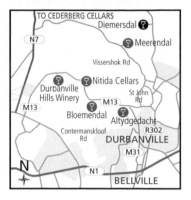

Stellenbosch & Somerset West region

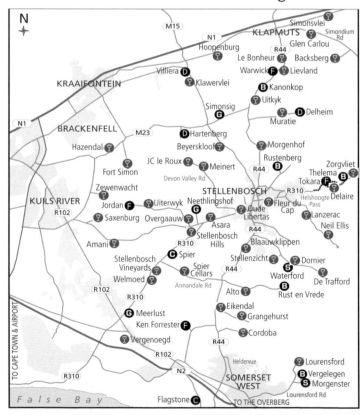

Franschhoek region

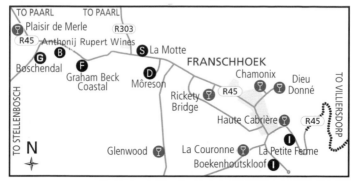

Overberg region (detail)

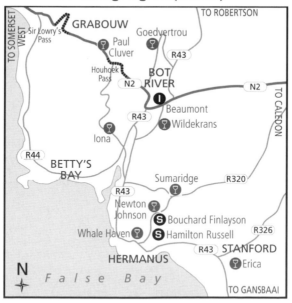

Paarl & Wellington region

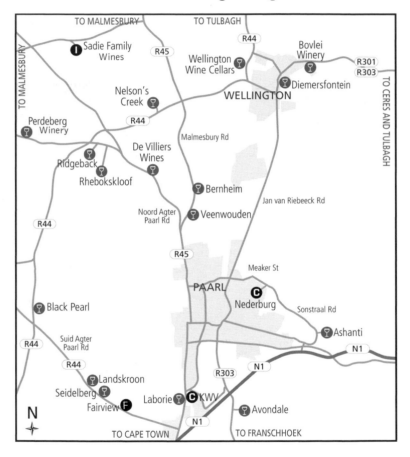

Robertson region

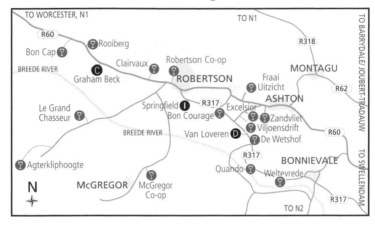

Worcester region

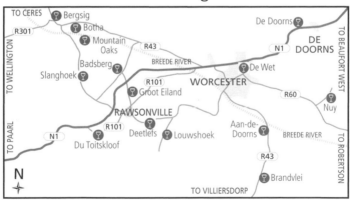

INTRODUCTION

The Quest

Travelling is not only about moving from one place to another: it can also be the state of seeking. You travel to find a place or you travel to find people. You seek out experiences and you look for something new. This is a book about travelling to find wines, because finding a new wine to enjoy means so much more than simply opening a different bottle.

Wine contains the spirit of a place – it's a natural combination of sunlight and soil and plant – but it also carries the mark of the humans who have interpreted the vine and made decisions in the cellar to shape the nature of the grape into wine of a certain character. Like a human, wine is some measure nature, some measure nurture – the first carrying the greater weight, but the second not to be discounted.

Wine embodies the signs of the place and culture it comes from – it's an expression of these forces, like music or painting. It's also an agricultural product, but with the emphasis on cultural, as in agri-*cultural*. And in this way wine can also be art. It interprets the world and the people in that world – another great reason to set off on a quest. You can say you're off to discover some living art …

Furthermore, searching, travelling and wine are natural

companions because making wine is also a quest; it's not a sprint around a racetrack but a trek into endless mountain ranges. It takes many years – even generations – to create good wine. There are few short cuts when it comes to making fine wine; nature rewards the steadfast.

But we aren't the winemakers, so a few short cuts would be useful … and that's exactly what you have in your hands. As you travel into the hills where the wines of the Cape are made, this guide will help you find the interesting spots and suggest a good few starting points.

The Cape is undeniably beautiful. To go looking for the places where wine is made will take you to some of the most beautiful areas of this spectacular region. Along the way you are likely to meet some great people – people who have dedicated their lives to the transformation of the grape into a complex, satisfying liquid; something with a life of its own that could exceed that of the maker; a drink that changes over the years; a living thing.

And don't forget: where you find wine, you find food. Often the best food of the region, because people who care about wine are very likely to care, just that little bit more, about food.

So let's be clear on one thing: Wine is not a drink like any other, and no one wine is like another. It's ever-changing and often challenging. Try them all and try not to have your mind made up before you do.

This book is your guide for questing into the winelands of the Cape. It is not designed to take you everywhere or explain everything, but rather to help get you on your way, to introduce you to the character of some of the places and describe various directions for you to explore according to your fancy – because if there is one truth about wine, it's that wine can be an endless quest, always changing, always fascinating. A lot like life.

The People You'll Meet

The people who make wine start with the oenologist, the highfalutin name for the winemaker who sculpts the wine, employing science to greater or lesser degrees. At one end, this is a highly trained technician with a deep understanding of the chemistry involved; with access to the inner secrets of the fruit of *Vitis vinifera* as it turns from little green berries into wine with a certain pH, level of acidity, and alcohol content.

At the other end, this is a farmer with an instinctive knack for turning the grapes into wine. Most are clearly a happy blend of the two; this would be your regular winemaker. If you meet these men and women on your travels you can really get to the heart of the matter, as this typical conversation illustrates:

Traveller: I really like this wine; how did you get it so good?

Winemaker: Well, if you start with perfect grapes, it's easy. Then you just guide the grapes through the cellar and do as little as possible.

Traveller: OK. But how do you know when the grapes are perfect?

Winemaker: Well, you look for optimal ripeness.

Traveller: How do you decide on this?

Winemaker: You'll have to speak to the viticulturist. To do with the colour of the pips and satellite imagery. But I just taste the grape and I know.

Traveller: Oh. Well, I really like this wine.

Winemaker (looks pleased and/or mysterious): Well, this really was the best vintage in recent memory. Perfect ripening conditions. (This, you will soon discover, is what they say every year.)

The winemaker has let on that he or she has some expert help in the form of the viticulturist, who tends to the vineyards and is rarely seen. This is the person carrying the awful responsibility of delivering this perfect grape, a nerve-racking gamble with nature.

If you meet one of these, they are likely to have a great deal more to say (they don't get much chance to talk about their work) but it is also likely to be even more difficult to understand than the winemaker's explanations. Terms like 'soil structure', 'water stress' and 'canopy management' sound technical even before you begin to try to understand them. This is deep geek territory with many conflicting theories. It's best avoided, which also explains why not too many people talk to the viticulturist or bring him or her to the wine dinners.

In the Cape, the winemaker and viticulturist have historically been rugged, big men, mostly of an Afrikaans persuasion and with a strong likelihood of having played as rugby forwards. While these amiable giants with huge forearms still make up a large proportion of the team, times have changed. You are as likely to meet a scrawny youth with a thousand-yard stare (from squinting into the sun looking for surf), or one of many female winemakers. But you are unlikely to encounter these key players as a matter of course. They are especially scarce during harvest times and, when sighted, look just like hobo-zombies dressed in red-stained rags – this due to the relentless lack of sleep and hours of grape-on-skin contact. Dishevelled winemakers have been known to fall asleep in their bowl of soup and many nascent relationships founder on the jagged rocks of harvest hours.

You are more likely to encounter, at the modern Cape winery, the front of house sales/tasting team. They range from a grandmotherly figure – often the mother or aunt of the winemaker, who has quietly stepped in to save the day – to very perky young women who will happily quote the salient facts and figures of how long the wine spent in wood, what food it is good with, and what the price is after tax. Shipping to Adelaide, Baden-Baden or Chattanooga? No problem.

There are also, unfortunately, a number of friendly but untrained tasting room staff still to be found. This guide gives you an indication of the all-round quality of your tasting experience with the ★ icon, and also an idea of how expensive the wines are with the $ icon. One of the joys of visiting the wineries is that the wines are often better priced at the cellar door.

You will see little of the dozens of hard workers behind the scenes who tend the vines and graft in the cellar. These oft-unsung heroes are nobly helping to guide tons and tons of grapes into becoming wine. Making wine is a fantastically demanding activity. Every vine is grown, trellised, pruned, picked, sprayed; bunches of grapes are hand-picked, individual grapes are sorted, and the berries are guided through the winery very gently. The resultant wine is mollycoddled over a number of years in steel and wood before being carefully bottled to arrive in front of you in pretty packaging.

> ♦ Note: Expect to pay a nominal fee for tastings; the days of free tastings are (mostly) gone, sad as it is (especially for the students).

Tasting facilities:

★   Not particularly well
             prepared for visitors;
             service is average
★ ★   A decent tasting area with
             helpful service
★ ★ ★   A great place to taste wine
             with good facilities and
             often a restaurant

Prices:

$ Inexpensive
$ $ Moderate
$ $ $ Expensive

The Lie of the Land

There is no other city in the world like Cape Town with such close access to such a fantastically diverse topography – much of it dedicated to the vine. The Western Cape really is wine country. In the days when the Cape was a refuelling station for passing ships and a garden was planted for supplies, the vine was one of the first plants to appear. Very soon the colonial bigwigs (literally – those Dutch colonialists had a taste for powdered wigs) had large vineyards, especially around the Constantia area and later in the prime winelands around Stellenbosch. The latter is in fact named after a primo bigwig, Simon van der Stel, and the 'bosch' or bush was quickly replaced by vines. As new settlers arrived, more areas took on vines, famously Franschhoek (French Corner), where the Huguenots settled.

Today, around 110 000 hectares of the Cape is under vine. We have the ideal climate, sitting smack bang in the Mediterranean latitudinal band that vines prefer. Another reason that the Cape is such a good wine-growing area is the wild diversity of the terrain, thanks to the many mountains and valleys that allow vines to find their ideal aspect; we also have a useful variety of soil types.

This geographic diversity also means that the Cape winelands are spectacular to travel through, a lush magnet for tourism.

It's all too heavenly – but then you do have Cape weather. Winemakers speak of the vines being cooled by the 'sea breezes' from the relatively close ocean, except that these cool breezes are often gales emanating from a sea that is brutally cold.

If it weren't for the searing frigidity of the waters and the relentlessness of the summer wind (the South-Easter), the Cape would be heaven for humans as well as vines.

But the beautiful Cape is mates with rugged, fickle weather, the type that likes to catch you out by changing quickly – and often. Like so many things in life, however, this lends character to the place. Life is most certainly not dull here.

The particularities of the weather also shape the vines. They have to put up a bit of a fight for life, and in this struggle they develop personalities that reflect the place and the weather. And it's these challenged vines that create good wines, not your lazy, couch-potato ones.

Due to the incredible natural diversity of the terrain, the wine areas of the Cape have been divided into regions, districts and wards to indicate their origin more precisely and to differentiate between areas that have noticeably different soils, topography and weather. Wine routes have sprung up within these divisions to celebrate the uniqueness of the areas and for each to brag about how they are, in fact, the best. One way to travel the winelands is according to these regions.

We'll rather be travelling according to the nature of the wineries themselves, their intrinsic character, be they large and loud, or hardy, compact individualists. For as important as place is (what is termed 'terroir' by the French), the human imprint is vital and lends a distinct personality to each winery.

According to your preferences, choose where to start using this book, with the characters you associate with, or ones you'd like to get to know better. These are entry points for your further exploration. Or travel not according to the wines and wineries, but all the other activities and interests that the winelands offer. You'll find these in the second section of the book.

The Wines

The soul of this quest, apart from the beautiful places we'll see and the friendly locals we hope to meet, is the wine. Let us never forget the wine. Though it will introduce many other angles and aspects of the Cape wine scene, this guide will always take you to places where the wines are worth the trip. The wineries that are described are first and foremost also makers of good wine – within a style or price point. Of course, 'good' is very relative when it comes to wine. (See page 160: What is a good wine?) Maybe we'll settle for calling them interesting, or wines of character and potential.

What makes the Cape winelands different?

Diversity. Drama. Tradition and innovation. Beauty. The Cape is often called a 'New World' wine region, meaning that we are not European, with many thousands of years of winemaking behind us. On the other hand, we do have 300-odd years under our belts and some pretty striking old estate houses with a very European flavour. The Cape is a fascinating mélange of the old and the new, with rapid changes having taken place in the 1990s to bring us up to speed with the modern wine world. There are few other places in the world where you can so quickly move between such different-looking spaces and experience such diversity in geography and culture. It is often remarked that our wines show a balance between the restraint of the European wines and the youthfulness and bold flavours of our New World companions, the Americas and Australasia. The Cape is still a meeting place of natural forces, travellers – and wine.

The Building Blocks

What Makes Wine? Fruit flavours, tannins and acidity.

These are the basic building blocks of wine – they could also be the sections of a band that work together to create music of one kind or another.

Fruit flavours are the singers or the solo instruments. They should be accomplished (ripe enough, developed enough) so that they put on a good show, but we don't want pastiche (overripeness) unless you are into cabaret or Liberace. Fruit flavours are mainly found in the skin of the grape.

Tannins are the rhythm section, the drums and bass: they set the beat. If they're too bold or loud, the fruit's voice is drowned out. Tannins come from the grape skins, pips, and (less and less in modern winemaking) from the stalks. These are the bass notes. Then there are the bold tannins from the wood used to mature the wine, in oak casks or with oak staves or chips (more cost-effective than the casks, but generally less sophisticated and less integrated into the wine flavours). These would be the drums.

Acidity is the volume of the music, and its reverberation – how long it lasts. Acidity is found in the grape in its natural form. In the Cape, many winemakers also add acid to give length to the wine when their grapes are too soft, i.e. not singing loudly enough. If this is done injudiciously, they are strident and hurt the proverbial ears (the mouth).

Red Wine Varieties

Cabernet Franc is the leaner and more acidic counterpart to Cabernet Sauvignon, though there are a number of Cape stand-alones that are very good. Marked by a leafy smell and intriguing spice notes, this is quite an intellectual wine. It is said to show terroir (see page 172) well.

Cabernet Sauvignon is the king of the grapes, complex and versatile, and can stand alone or work in a blend, traditionally with Merlot and Cabernet Franc, more innovatively with Shiraz or Pinotage. Cabernet has a good tannin structure which means it ages well; it's the backbone of a good wine and its dense flavour profile is in the dark fruit zone: blackberries and blackcurrant. Goes well with rich foods.

Merlot is a softer grape, with gentler tannins, but often a leaner structure than Cabernet. Its flavours tend also to black fruits, but with the added nuances of mocha and fruitcake and sometimes a mineral earthiness that can add great complexity to a blend. Called a 'feminine' red in some circles.

Pinotage is our home-grown cross of Pinot Noir and Cinsaut. It's a hearty wine with big structure and often expressive boiled sweet tones; sometimes sweet banana flavours can be detected. It's now often used as a small part of a red blend. This wine is a good companion for the traditional South African braai (barbecue).

Pinot Noir in the Cape makes a fuller wine than any Burgundian expression, though it is generally still a lighter wine than other reds (and not loved by macho men). Pinot has a strawberry liveliness, also black cherry, with an underlying power that's referred to as the 'iron fist in the velvet glove'. Partners lamb particularly well.

Shiraz (or Syrah) is a flavourful and expressive grape that's associated with spiciness, smoke and rich, earthy notes; sometimes sweetish. In the Cape, where it is becoming more and more popular, it is often made in a very rich (alcoholic) style, when the grape gets huge dark berry flavours and sometimes a cola tone. Great with grilled meats.

White Wine Varieties

Chardonnay is still the king of the whites, even though there is an opposition ABC (Anything But Chardonnay) camp. People still love its citrus notes and florals with the buttery/toasty layers that come from considered wood maturation. Can age well, and is good with food.

Chenin Blanc is a superbly versatile grape that makes anything from sparkling wine to table wine to 'stickies' – the sweet wines. We have lots of it planted in the Cape and it makes attractive melon- and peach-fruited wines. The wooded ones gain complexity and great honeyed richness (these for creamy dishes). A worthy Cape calling card.

Riesling, possibly the noblest white grape in terms of its ageing potential, has suffered from the image problem of being seen only as a sweet wine (though it does make the best sweet wines). Those days are over and there are great examples of its crisp apple and spicy character around. It can gain an interesting petroleum whiff when it ages. A versatile food partner, try with light meats, white sauces and rich salads.

Sauvignon Blanc is currently the highly fashionable white: zippy and zesty and bright. It can be tropical and sweetish, or dry and racy with green vegetal characters. The best examples also show some mineral tones. Great with fish dishes.

Sémillon is gaining some ground in the Cape, a super-grassy wine that can be very expressive and makes bold, limey wines, broader in flavour than Sauvignon Blanc. Works well with wood, too, and is a natural blend with Sauvignon Blanc.

Three best tips to improve your wine appreciation

- Drink from a biggish glass and fill to only a third of the way up.

- If you are tasting more than one wine, eat green olives in between to keep your palate sharp.

- Drink your older wines before the younger ones. They're usually more quietly complex, plus you'll give them the attention they deserve.

GRANDES DAMES

'New nobility is but the act of power, but ancient nobility is the act of time.'

– *Francis Bacon*

When the Dutch and French settlers found the Cape to their liking, a few of the big men decided to knock up local incarnations of European homes in a style befitting their important status. These houses, with their elaborate gables, whitewashed walls, thatched roofs, sprawling outhouses and many hectares of land have become the guidebook icons of the Cape winelands, and an essential image of South Africa as a whole. The combination of striking vernacular architecture set against jagged mountains with serried vines running out front creates a delightful and eternally appealing panorama.

Besides this natural beauty, what makes these farms Grandes is their reputation as makers of fine wines; Dames because they have centuries of heritage but carry it lightly. With reputations as old as the Cape wine scene, the Grandes Dames are most people's first introduction to the wines of the Cape. As you can appreciate, being the symbol of a whole country has shaped the character of these estates. Like the gabled heerenhuise (Gentlemen's Houses) themselves, the farms are stately and tranquil. The yellowwood floors of the homes creak comfortably, carrying the weight of years with grace.

In gentler ages, it used to be easier to ride on centuries of good repute, but the Dames have, in modern times, had to shake a leg on the vinous front to stay in the game. Of course this is something that needed to be achieved without disrupting their gracious demeanour. Grandes Dames aren't into change for the thrill of it. A certain conservatism, call it reserve, is part of their charm, and their wines often reflect this.

The accumulation of time means that a large variety of wines are typically made at these estates, the many grandchildren of a materfamilias. Cabernet Sauvignon and Chardonnay, those most venerable of grapes, are favourites because they are 'noble' varieties (see page 29). A late harvested wine is often part of the family, preferably a noble late harvest wine. Another salient feature, in this age that celebrates the individual (in the case of wine this would be the winemaker), is the more European approach of the Grandes Dames in keeping this crucial but transient person out of the limelight; the wines are about the (relatively) ageless estate more than the human caretakers.

Still, a side effect of these more dishevelled times is that the Grandes Dames, traditionally family-run, are becoming businesses, with restaurants, tours of the estate and manor and souvenir shops – they offer much more than just wine to the guest. Which is just as well, it's our time now, us commoners, and it's a real treat to get a look in to how the other half used to live.

Groot Constantia Estate

Cherry-picked by the Dutch Guv'nor Simon van der Stel as his personal spread, and so the oldest official farm in the Cape (1685), Groot Constantia Estate has history in spades. Incredibly, wines have been made here since 1688 and the sweet wines of the eighteenth and nineteenth century (as approved by Napoleon and Jane Austen) were world famous, as was the eccentric owner Hendrik Cloete, who preferred to be roused from his slumbers by a musical quartet playing outside his bedroom window. Talk about a gentler time. Today the majesty of this fine living has been preserved on the farm with its collection of historic buildings and pretty gardens. Indeed, the farm has been converted into a museum estate with important collections of furniture from bygone eras in the manor house and the original cellar. In keeping with this famous estate's place in Cape wine history, a ceremony to mark 350 years of Cape winemaking was held here in 2009.

Constantia Road, Constantia
(021) 794-5128
Mon-Sun 9am-6pm
(5pm May-Nov)
Facilities ★ ★ ★
Prices $$

The exteriors of the buildings are works of art themselves, and the old wine cellar features some striking allegorical frescoes on its facade. It's worth the visit just to stroll around the grounds and then sit under the oaks for scones and tea or a heartier meal from one of the two restaurants on the property. (But go at off-peak times if you are allergic to big groups.)

For all her charms, this Dame is still a fully operational wine farm, and – as the wine tasting and estate tours facility at the entrance will attest – she is market-savvy. If you are in a hurry and just want a few wines with this famous label to take home, the shop at the entrance has all these and curios too, but you won't see anything of the original homestead up the hill, which would be a shame.

A big range of wines has always been made here: reds, whites, blends, bubblies and ports. This catholic variety is still in evidence, but, in line with the trend to concision, it's slowly being focused to concentrate on the 'noble' varieties. There has been considerable energy spent on upgrading the vineyards for wine quality, not just to continue to look as photogenic as they always do.

● pick of the wines

The wines with the name 'Gouverneur's Reserve' are the top tier, and in general they are a few notches up in quality. The Gouverneur's Reserve Merlot is an estate triumph in a heavy, rich style. The Gouverneur's Reserve is the Bordeaux-style blend, packed with fresh fruit flavours in a New World style.

while in the area

Do

- Visit the manor house museum if you have an interest in how the other half used to live in times gone by, and to feel an aura of history.
- Walk up the garden lane to the historic bath.

Eat

* Simon's Restaurant has great views, alfresco dining and modern, fresh food (021) 794-1143; the Jonkerhuis features Cape Malay and traditional plates in comfortable and warm bistro environment; picnics also available if you call ahead (021) 794-6255.

Meerlust Estate

The thing about having the Grandes Dames' centuries of heritage is that, if you build on repeated success, you establish a legendary reputation that's unassailably buttressed by history. One such true Cape icon, tried and tested in the age-old tradition, is Meerlust Estate. This stately farm has over time become bigger than the people, even though many generations of the Myburgh family have lived here.

On R310 (off N2 to Stellenbosch)
(021) 843-3587
Sales: Mon-Fri 9am-5pm, Sat 10am-2pm
Facilities ★ ★ ★
Prices $$$

Meerlust was not always on the Cape's fine wines map, though there have always been vines planted here. People may occupy transient spaces in time relative to estates, but tradition is built by those who understand and appreciate legacy and prevail in the face of time's many challenges: and so it was that, around 1950, Nico Myburgh began reshaping the farm with a firm and considered view to making fine wine. His son Hannes today continues to steer the wines along their now-established path of great renown.

Crucially, too, Meerlust honours tradition in the cellar, and the winemakers appreciate those who have gone before. Italian-born Giorgio Dalla Cia took the helm from 1978 to 2003, making wine along time-honoured French lines with utmost confidence: 'I don't see why I should change an approach that's worked for centuries.' Working only with the classic French varieties, Dalla Cia was among the first Cape winemakers to blend Cabernet Sauvignon, Merlot and Cabernet Franc to make a Bordeaux-style blend called Rubicon. Now there is new blood in the cellar, and the aim of Chris Williams (who did an apprenticeship under Dalla Cia) is further refinement: 'to discover the true personality of Meerlust', is how he puts it.

Meerlust Estate is perhaps most famous for its Chardonnay. This wine was first released in 1995, after more than a decade of experimentation. Who other than a Grande Dame would have the time, the ability and, above all, the philosophical gumption to do this? To take a decade to groom your wine and all the while resist the pressures of commercialism takes, shall we say, a historic view on time.

In this spirit, the wines of Meerlust Estate are created to be aged. The red wines are released a full four years after harvest, instead of the usual two. In a world where wine is typically drunk on the day of purchase, this respectable on-farm maturation presents the wine in a much better light and encourages the habit of maturing good reds. You could argue that this is a luxury that comes of many years of production, but it is also a statement of a belief: wines are the products of time and need time to express their true character. Meerlust takes its time, and has gathered a three-century-old scrapbook as a result.

◖ pick of the wines

Justly famed for the Rubicon, a poised and august wine, and their finessed Chardonnay, the estate also makes a polished Pinot Noir Reserve and a voluptuous Merlot. All these wines are built for the long haul, with layered tannins (for lovers of good oak) and elegance.

while in the area

Do

* Visit neighbouring Vergenoegd for another very historic winery and the good Pomegranate restaurant (021) 843-3248 through which you could see the vineyard ducks troop.

Boschendal Wines

Synonymous with summer picnics and a shining star on the Cape tourist track, this Dame does not disappoint. There's an iconic manor house to explore, a delightful tasting venue under ancient oaks, a gift shop, sprawling gardens and lawns galore, two restaurants, a stone sculpture garden and a famous, huge picnic

R310 on the Franschhoek side
(021) 870-4211
May-Oct: Mon-Sat 8.30am-4.30pm, Nov-Apr: Mon-Sun 8.30am-4.30pm
Facilities ★ ★ ★
Prices $ to $$

area. The ducks that come begging for your breadcrumbs add the farmyard authenticity (and interestingly duck is on the menu too ...).

Boschendal ('bush and dale') was one of the original farms granted to the French Huguenot settlers when they arrived in the Cape towards to the end of the seventeenth century. In its early days it rose to become a model farm under the ownership of the De Villiers family, but its centuries of wine-making history were curtailed by the devastation of phylloxera (a vine louse) in the late nineteenth century. It was then bought by the mining magnate Cecil John Rhodes (who bought many of the neighbouring farms in this Drakenstein valley) and transformed into a successful fruit farm. Over the years, and under the stewardship of the Anglo American Corporation, vines were reintroduced.

By the early 1980s, Boschendal was again one of the grandest Dames in the winelands. The manor house had been splendidly restored, the gardens were world famous. The picnic on its lawns was a must-do, and the restaurant was one of the best in the Cape. The cellar also produced a rosé wine that became a mega-hit and the spearhead for all the other wines (and continues to seduce to this day). And so it was that this Grande Dame was rapidly transformed into a public playground – one of the prettiest and most hospitable around.

As inappropriate as it is for a Dame to be so inconvenienced, she was sold in 2003, and there are plans to develop some of her large grounds into a boutique hotel and private estates, but Boschendal's famous hospitality will continue. During these latter years, her cellar has also undergone a period of reinvigoration and innovation with new wine ranges coming on stream, including the commemorative Cecil John Reserve range.

🍾 pick of the wines

Boschendal makes a wide selection of wines – something to suit all palates and pockets. At the top, the Cecil John Sauvignon Blanc is a pure and intense example of the variety, while the stablemate Shiraz is a big and powerful wine of stature. The Grand Reserve is a fine blend, and at the budget end the La Pavillion white and red are perfect for picnics or casual dinners at home.

while in the area

Do

+ Avoid big groups, go at off-peak times and wander through the herb and rose gardens, then up the oaks to the picnic lawns.
+ Visit the fantastically curated museum, in the old manor house.

Eat

+ A basket and a few friends is the perfect way to taste the wide variety of wines they produce. During the summer season there are also full moon picnics ...
+ Or visit one of the two restaurants on the property; the Boschendal Restaurant is a great place to taste old-style Cape cooking. Lunch daily (021) 870 4274.

Other
Noteworthy
Grandes Dames

Klein Constantia Estate

Back in the day, when Governor Van der Stel and Hendrik Cloete owned Constantia, there was no distinction between Groot and Klein Constantia, but in 1819 the big spread was divided, and today Klein Constantia may be small in name, but it is big in winemaking

Constantia Road, Constantia
(021) 794-5188
Mon-Fri 9-5; Sat 9-1pm
Facilities ★
Prices $$ to $$$

reputation. This is due to the custodianship of the Jooste family and their reintroduction, in the 1980s, of Vin de Constance, a sweet wine made in the style of the world-famous Constantia wines of the eighteenth and nineteenth centuries.

These wines of Constantia were famous for their ability to age. At the end of the twentieth century, a few bottles of vintage 1791 were discovered and tasted – incredibly the wine still glowed with life. This was, after all, the wine that Napoleon begged for while in exile, and as it proved, they sure were good enough to make again. Since the reintroduction of the Vin de Constance, it has quickly become one of the world's must-try wines.

Klein Constantia Estate has its own share of natural beauty, tucked into a glade against the mountain, and it has its own delightful collection of historic buildings, including a pretty mosque. Ross Gower made some fantastic white wines here in the latter part of the twentieth century and was instrumental in the reintroduction of Vin de Constance. Adam Mason took over the reins in 2003, during a time of substantial vineyard reinvigoration and the reintroduction of their red wines. Sauvignon Blanc is the other leading light here, the mountainous slopes and sea-facing vines being ideal for making crystalline styles of this white wine.

pick of the wines

U ndoubtedly the Vin de Constance is a must, but all the wines here are of a fine quality. The single vineyard 'Perdeblokke' Sauvignon Blanc is really special, very elegant and refined; and their Rhine Riesling is dry and mineral. For a more day-to-day tipple, the KC Cabernet Sauvignon-Merlot is lovely.

Buitenverwachting

I t's fitting that the team at Buitenverwachting is headed up by a very urbane European, Lars Maack. He has in common with the estate the courteousness and civility that this Grande Dame in Constantia exudes, with its

Off the Spaanschemat River Road, M42, Constantia
(021) 794-5190
Mon-Fri 9am-5pm, Sat 9am-1pm
Facilities ★★★
Prices $$

ancient trees, horses in the paddocks and views out over the city. It's all very genteel and well bred. Well bred can of course be awfully stiff. Not here. The name Buitenverwachting means 'beyond expectations' and applies neatly to the way the estate carries class without fustiness.

When it comes to wine, the hallmark of the Grandes Dames is consistency. It's no accident that the winemaker here, Hermann Kirschbaum, has been in the cellar for over a decade. Good winemaking is essentially a conservative pastime, one that happens at the pace of seasons, and it rewards those who show a tenacity of attention and meticulousness. Their approach to wine echoes the European ideals of balance and suppleness as opposed to brash, strident flavours, and Buitenverwachting's wines are welcome examples of drinkability in the face of the overly manipulated jungle juice that is sometimes called 'wine'.

Choosing not to chase fashion is the natural state for a Grande Dame. Yet they are pacesetters in many respects: like the consistency that results in wines that almost every restaurant lists – from the light 'pop idol' Buiten Blanc, to the Bordeaux-style blend diva, Christine. The abilities to hop between the frivolous and the serious and to carry experience and sophistication lightly are accomplishments that can't be learnt in a hurry.

🍷 pick of the wines

Christine, the Bordeaux-style blend, is one of the more austere wines around, filled with charms but not likely to reveal them too quickly – a true Grande Dame trait. The Chardonnay is another wine of class and reserved distinction. On the other end of the spectrum, Buiten Blanc is a likely contender for the most successful and popular blended white in the land, but still not just a simple wine.

Simonsig Wine Estate

At this Grande Dame, the Cape Dutch homestead is out of sight and still used as a home, but the tasting area recreates the 'olde' feel. This Dame is family-owned, the brothers Malan forging ahead on the legacy of their father, Frans. Frans Malan was a key figure in making the Cape wineries tourist

Kromme Rhee Road,
Koelenhof, between R44
& R304
(021) 888-4900
Mon-Fri 8.30am-5pm,
Sat 8.30am-4pm
Facilities ★ ★
Prices $ to $$

friendly by being a founder of the Stellenbosch wine route. He was also a pioneer in the revival of sparkling wine in the French method (here called Méthode Cap Classique) with their popular Kaapse Vonkel in the 1970s. Now the workload is split between his three sons, the viticulturist, winemaker and marketing manager, respectively. You don't get better division of labour.

Simonsig Wine Estate is still an incredibly tourist friendly winery with its big tasting room and knowledgeable help. There's a feeling of lively, relaxed history here, no mothballs or pretences. There's even a children's park and a vineyard garden so that you can be introduced to the vine that produces your favourite wine; while the on-site Cuvée restaurant serves good modern interpretations of traditional Cape cuisine.

As is the habit of Grandes Dames, there used to be a sumptuous variety of vines spread across the big properties. In recent years the brothers have been working on cutting this plethora down to move into a higher quality gear. Still, there's an impressive range. True to the Cape heritage that the farm represents, pinotage takes pride of place, both as a single variety and in a flagship blend, the Frans Malan.

🍾 pick of the wines

The Frans Malan makes a loud shout for the rightful place for pinotage – in a blend. A big, expressive wine. The Merindol Syrah is another banner wine, and priced as such, very powerful, though no rough edges. Their sparklers are always superb, led by the Cuvée Royale, while the Kaapse Vonkel remains an honest-priced favourite.

The Noble Lot

Even in grape varieties there are those that are noble and those that are 'less equal'. Another word for the noble varieties is 'classic'. These are the vines that historically (in other words, in France, the cradle of wine tradition) were considered superior due to their smaller, more concentrated berries – better for quality wine production. The reds include Cabernet Sauvignon, Merlot, Pinot Noir and Cabernet Franc; the whites Chardonnay and Riesling. With the opening up of new wine territories and their specific climates, and, with other varieties employed that are better suited to them, there has been some revising of this hierarchy. Still, a certain cachet yet surrounds this royal family.

BIG HITTERS

'At the age of six I wanted to be a cook. At seven I wanted to be Napoleon. And my ambition has been growing steadily ever since.'

– Salvador Dali

The Big Hitters can be very close to the Grandes Dames in character. Their differences usually revolve around fine distinctions, because the Dames are also big in reputation, after all. Many Big Hitters also share with Grandes Dames the traditional Cape Dutch spreads and beautiful grounds: the makings of genteel confidence.

The key difference is to be found in a certain exuberance of personality – an extroversion – that goes hand in hand with the Big Hitter's winning way in the matter of the successful marketing of their fine wines. Big Hitters don't mind bragging, but their names are usually promoted by a combination of class, quality and a good track record. The wines they make speak for themselves. But well turned-out marketing reps certainly help. Big Hitters have decided to be more assertive in their talents, more expressive in their desire to make some of the best wines in the world. They haven't waited for it to come to them: they've shone their stylish Italian leather shoes and gone out looking. The world's stage is where they belong.

These are the wineries that are most likely to be polled the best in the Cape, to make any top ten list, and be the darlings of the wine competitions. Their consistency ensures that it's certainly not just flash; they have all the intrinsic quality to beat the best in the world, and good track records to boot. These aren't small boutique wineries either, so the ability to make decent quantities of wine of this quality speaks of attention to detail and the willingness to go to whatever lengths it takes – only the best is good enough.

And while their reputations are founded on top wines, they also flaunt their figureheads, usually the winemaker but just as easily the owner, who is usually something of a star and not at all shy of publicity.

Marketing know-how and a confidence in product does make for premium wines, but they have no problem selling what they make – they are the 'made men' of the winelands and could be considered the Cape's 'first growth' wineries (see page 170). So, if you prefer your wine with a bit of swagger and prefer flashing a label that makes a statement, these are the guys for you. Your arrival at a party with one of their bottles is sure to be warmly greeted.

Rust en Vrede Estate

Rust en Vrede means 'tranquillity and peacefulness', delights which translate perfectly to the successful vinification of fine red wines – specifically their languid ageing in expensive French oak casks and later in expensive high-quality bottles – these being hallmark features of Stellenbosch's stylish Rust en Vrede.

Annandale Road, Stellenbosch
(021) 881-3881
Mon-Fri 9am-5pm, Sat 9am-4pm (3pm in winter)
Facilities ★ ★ ★
Prices $$ to $$$

Jean Engelbrecht is congenitally geared to be a Big Hitter. His father Jannie Engelbrecht achieved folk hero status as a

Springbok rugby player before buying this attractive historic farm to make his first wine in 1979, in a cellar that was one of the first private operations to boast an underground maturation facility. Before long, he was making only red wines – as befits the image of a lusty, lively, robust character – though remember that red is also the colour of the wine thinker, the one willing to work over time, with patience.

Son Jean also followed a rather macho career (as an airline pilot) before taking the reins of the family farm. And take them he has. Today, Rust en Vrede Estate is even bigger in repute, making solely red wines, with a knack for Shiraz and a fine estate red blend. And speaking of big hitters, Jean Engelbrecht teamed up with the Big Easy, golfer Ernie Els, to establish Ernie Els Wines in 2000, another cellar dedicated to bold reds. (They're also partners in the affiliated Guardian Peak winery, all in the same valley.) To round out the luxurious experience that Rust en Vrede embodies, they opened an eponymous restaurant on the farm in 2007 and it's rapidly established itself as one of the best in the world, never mind just the Cape winelands.

Engelbrecht and quietly spoken winemaker Coenie Snyman are intensely focused on maintaining their 'first growth' red status through a range of wines that are undeniably New World in structure. Rust en Vrede reds are bold and svelte, pretty outgoing, with oodles of lavish character, and are certainly not strangers to judges' awards, particularly in the United States of America where, as they say, big is beautiful. While their wines are large and generous, it would be a mistake to assume that they lack finesse; these giants have their soft side and have no lack of sophistication. They're a lot like the place: a combination of grace and grandeur.

🍾 pick of the wines

Rust en Vrede Estate is the wine that contains all the power and grace of this aristocratic farm; it is recognised as a Cape wine benchmark. However, any wine that you encounter with this farm's name on it is worth a look. A recent addition to the range is the '1694' – a powerful blend of Shiraz and Cabernet Sauvignon, aged in both French and American oak. The Ernie Els is a substantial Bordeaux-style blend of good breeding; while their explorations with younger vines and other (off estate) vineyards in the Guardian Peak range are rewarding – especially the Shiraz-Mourvèdre-Grenache or SMG – yet another winning example of this winery's penchant for the blend.

While in the area

Do

- The farm is a nature conservancy and a few walks in the pretty valley are signposted.
- The quaint farm stall around the corner on the main road is stocked with local dried fruits and curios as well as a great wine selection – and they have strawberry picking in season. Mooiberge Farm Stall, on the R44 (021) 881-3222.

Eat

- At the fine diner on the estate. Chef David Higgs cooks world-class modern cuisine (dinner only) but you can have a one-plate vintner's lunch during the week.

Rustenberg Wines

Established in 1682, and making wine soon after. You'd be hard-pressed to find a more beautiful location anchored by a more famous Cape Dutch building than this 1000-hectare plus estate. It was even once owned by the last prime minister of the Cape Colony in the

Rustenberg Road, Stellenbosch
(021) 809-1200
Mon-Fri 9am-4.30pm,
Sat 10am-1.30pm
(3.30pm in Dec/Jan)
Facilities ★ ★
Prices $$ to $$$

British colonial years, along with illustrious families like the Cloetes of Groot Constantia. Blue-blooded indeed.

Current owners, the Barlow family, bought the magnificent farm in 1941. A family of industrialists, Simon Barlow pulled out of the industrial sector in the mid-1980s to focus entirely on rebuilding Rustenberg, which is one of the longer-running wineries in South African history, having first sold estate-bottled wine in 1892.

The road to the farm doesn't suggest anything but bucolic reveries. The meandering road from the town of Stellenbosch to Rustenberg takes you through rural landscapes, scenes from a bygone era – and just when you think it cannot be more pastoral, you see their prize Jersey cow herd (in charge of milk supplies for the farm's cheese), and your vision of tranquillity is complete.

However, the modern tasting room and equally updated winery tell the other side of the story; of owner Simon Barlow's focus on the global playing field and the farm's comfort in Big Hitter territory. During the 1990s, he undertook a massive replanting of the vineyards and a resulting major leap in production took them to the forefront of South Africa's reintegration into world economies. The construction of a modern cellar came soon after to meld the time-honoured with the best of the new: tradition with progress. Barlow has also collected a team of young eccentrics to help him, people who straddle the divide between custom and the modern with aplomb and a great deal of humour. Nothing stiff or formal about this team.

Here the expectation of generations is carried lightly, but never irresponsibly. The flagship Peter Barlow Cabernet Sauvignon commemorates Simon's father who began the upgrading of the farm to take it from Grande Dame to Big Hitter; while the Brampton range is full of forward-looking innovation. Lesser known varieties like Rousanne, Marsanne and Carignan are being planted to liven blends up and make sure that tradition never becomes a straitjacket at this venerable property. It's an attitude that comes from Rustenberg's estate wines having been leaders in quality and stature for more than a century, with no sign of slacking off.

♦ pick of the wines

The Peter Barlow Cabernet Sauvignon and Five Soldiers Chardonnay are at the top of the Cape's A-list. Both are deeply structured wines with ample oaking for cellaring. The John X Merriman red blend doesn't pull its punches either, while the Brampton range's full fruit flavours are epitomised in the Viognier, a near impossibly rich (and strong) wine. The Brampton Old Vines Red (OVR) is great drinking and good value, as is the Brampton Shiraz.

while in the area

Do

- Buy some of the Jersey herd's delicious soft cheeses, on sale in the wine shop.
- Take the time to stroll around the premises and indulge in the daydream that you own a piece of it, or pretend you're in a Jane Austen novel.

Anthonij Rupert Wines

A vintage car casually parked at the gate of this estate hints that this is no ordinary entrance. Owned by Johann Rupert, head of (inter alia) the international Richemont group, Anthonij Rupert Wines certainly crumples ordinary and bins it.

On R45, Franschhoek
(021) 874-9000
Mon-Fri 9am-4.30pm,
Sat 10am-3pm
Facilities ★ ★ ★
Prices $$ to $$$

The original name of this estate, L'Ormarins, is well known to Cape wine lovers, for wine has been bottled under this name since 1982 (though wine was originally made here in the late eighteenth century). The early twenty-first century saw big changes. In 2004, a new cellar was built, and the whole farm closed in 2005 for a near-complete replanting programme. It went from hosting 550 hectares of vines to 110 hectares in a ruthless drive for correct varietal plantings. Where there used to be vines, on soil that is not really suited to it, there is now a world-class horse stud, and a fantastic motor car museum (thoroughbred horses and supercars – any doubt this is a Big Hitter?).

The new vineyard plantings are innovative. High density plantings, mixed trellising and experimental irrigation systems are the order of the day. And in the modern spirit of wider environmental integration, there is also a strong ecological component alongside the new plantings; the surrounding natural 'fynbos' vegetation has been extensively rehabilitated. As a result, the antelope have returned, also the eagles to catch the mice to catch the bugs – while dog hair in bags keeps the baboons at bay.

Then there is the new cellar. A jaw-dropping technological marvel, whole floors rotate at the press of a button. James Bond's Q would love it. Here, the Anthonij Rupert Wines range is made – the brand that now incorporates L'Ormarins, Terra del Capo and the Anthonij Rupert signature range. Grapes come from this farm as well as the family vineyards in the Swartland and Darling regions.

Visitors are taken by golf cart from the parking area to the tasting room (the old slave quarters) where the new fruits of a magnate's labour can be tasted. In keeping with the spirit of a Big Hitter, the flagship wines are no blushing brides. Not many people are happy to push the boundaries in terms of ripeness and balance, but here there is no fear. From these bold and ripe, lush beauties, named after types of indigenous vegetation, you move to the L'Ormarins wines that are more commercially tuned and on to the Italian-influenced Terra del Capo range – so something for most everyone.

'Ask the man who owns one' was a famous tagline for Packard motor cars in the day. This Big Hitter certainly shows you what a few rands and cents can conjure.

🍾 pick of the wines

Serruria is a Chardonnay made in a full oxidative, traditional style. It's a complex and luscious wine of immense depth. Nemesia is a white blend of Chenin Blanc, Chardonnay and Viognier that has vigorous energy and an attractively firm mineral core with lovely ripe fruit overlaid. L'Ormarins Optima is still a lovely red, generous fruit but properly dry and harnessed by lovely firm tannins in the classic style. Great food wine.

while in the area

Do

◆ Visit the fascinating Franschhoek Motor Museum on the property. Not only for petrolheads (though they'll drool). Tues-Sun 9am-4.30pm.

Eat

◆ Have lunch at nearby Vrede en Lust's Cotage Fromage, especially if you love cheese. 021 874-3991. Daily breakfast and lunch.

Other Noteworthy Big Hitters

Kanonkop Estate

Cannon Hill is an appropriate name for this red specialist – few others reverberate with its gravitas. There used to be a real cannon on the hill, a seventeenth-century early warning system to let farmers know of ships arriving in the bay for replenishment; today it's the symbol for another of the Cape's 'first growth' estates. The Paul Sauer

R44 between
Stellenbosch and
Klapmuts
(021) 884-4656
Mon-Fri 8.30am-5pm,
Sat 9am-12.30pm
Tours by appointment
Facilities ★★
Prices $$$

Bordeaux-style blend is legendary, but it is Kanonkop Estate's successes with South Africa's home-grown variety, Pinotage (see page 45), that have made this name world renowned.

Former winemaker Beyers Truter made it happen, he's an unflagging champion of Pinotage and probably the winemaker who knows the most about this national grape. The estate has 40 per cent of its vineyard area planted to Pinotage, some vines as old as fifty years, and in case there's any doubt about their favourite, their stylish and rather plush tasting room carries the following above the door: 'Pinotage is the juice extracted from women's tongues and lion's hearts. After having sufficient quantity, one can talk forever and fight the devil.'

These reds are made in a traditional manner: fermented in open containers, not the modern stainless steel. This allows for more skin contact and the result is wines that have great texture and mouthfeel, along with suppleness.

This combination of old vines, old technique and old money is an impressive one and, as you could expect, the wines are not cheap. The vintage on sale at the winery is always a little older than that of many other producers, to encourage drinking the wines when they are ready – the wines are made to mature beautifully.

ᵭ pick of the wines

The Kadette is their entry level red from younger vineyards; a friendlier price but no coward in flavour or the sophisticated, textured tannins that make their reds special. The Pinotage is about seriousness, not simple sweet fruit, like many examples of this wine. It usually needs a few years to express itself fully. The Cabernet Sauvignon oozes class, balance and plushness in one. Paul Sauer is the showstopper – and it invariably sells out within a week …

Thelema Mountain Vineyards

The exception proves the rule, and this Big Hitter doesn't have the accoutrements of historic buildings or paddocks. What it does share with the others is a huge reputation

R310 Helshoogte Pass
(021) 885-1924
Mon-Fri 9am-5pm, Sat 9am-1 pm
Facilities ★ ★
Prices $$ to $$$

for making iconic Cape wines that centres around owner/ cellarmaster Gyles Webb and his consistent knack for excellence.

While Webb is very self-effacing with his relaxed demeanour – another exception to the Big Hitter approach – Thelema, with its vineyards on high in the Helshoogte Pass, went on to rock the world with reds and whites that proved as drinkable as they were age-worthy.

Thelema continues to deliver the goods, and if you speak to any winemaker they will rave about Webb's attention to cutting edge vineyard practice as well as his 'manicured' vines. If any further proof that the route to good wines begins in the vineyard is needed, begin here. In fact, Webb always credits his good fortune to be working on these soils when describing the wine. In the cellar, he takes the 'Keep It Simple, Stupid' approach of minimal intervention, maintaining the hands-on/hand-made quality that his wines embody. This carries through to the remarkably relaxed and friendly tasting room – where most of the wines are unfortunately usually sold out.

It was the promise of the soils here that drew Gyles Webb, but you could be excused for coming to enjoy the exceptional view, with the shrieks of the local peacocks as your soundtrack.

pick of the wines

It's really up to you: all the wines are winners. The Merlot is one of the Cape's finest, while the Cabernet Sauvignon is an established classic. One of the best Rhine Rieslings, at a very good price, is also made here. Webb is developing vineyards in the new cool-climate winelands, Elgin, so expect Thelema to continue to maintain its vanguard character.

Vergelegen

The winery closest to its Grande Dame family tree is also the winery that's had the most impressive competitive track record of all in South Africa's new democracy years. Vergelegen is one of the original Cape farms, the personal spread of Dutch governor Willem

Lourensford Road,
Somerset West
(021) 874-1334
9.30am-4.30pm daily
and guided cellar tours
Facilities ★ ★ ★
Prices $$$

Adriaan van der Stel (son of Simon). Vines were first planted here in 1700.

Its name means 'far flung' (from the early settlement of Cape Town) but now it has been encroached by the suburban sprawl of Somerset West with a very fancy golfing estate right on its border. But the farm still has the mountainside and oodles of space. It remains one of the Cape's most beautiful natural and cultivated environments, with a manor house that's a jewel in the heritage crown (a tour of the magnificent house is included in the fee at the gate) and stunning gardens.

Then there is the wine. Anglo American bought the farm in the latter part of the twentieth century and asserted its world-conquering might – very intelligently – on the vineyards.

A few big-hitting blends, the red a two times winner of the trophy for the best blended red in the world and a sumptuous white blend lead the range. All the wines are models of intensity matched by balance: world-class in any circles.

It began its life as a model farm and this spirit certainly still lives on at Vergelegen today.

♦ pick of the wines

Besides the flagship red and white blends, both simply called Vergelegen, which have to be tasted if only for calibration purposes, the Cabernet Sauvignon is a superb example of Cape Cab. One of the Cape's best Sauvignon Blancs is also made here, in a 'standard' and reserve form: very limited and from a single vineyard area on the farm. Whatever your wine preference, the example here is worth a look. But be aware that you pay per wine to taste in the rather formal and serious tasting facility.

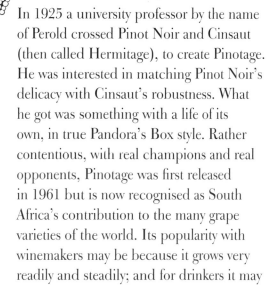

What's up with Pinotage?

In 1925 a university professor by the name of Perold crossed Pinot Noir and Cinsaut (then called Hermitage), to create Pinotage. He was interested in matching Pinot Noir's delicacy with Cinsaut's robustness. What he got was something with a life of its own, in true Pandora's Box style. Rather contentious, with real champions and real opponents, Pinotage was first released in 1961 but is now recognised as South Africa's contribution to the many grape varieties of the world. Its popularity with winemakers may be because it grows very readily and steadily; and for drinkers it may be for its expressive fruit flavours. Pinotage readily makes juicy easy-drinkers, but it's also a popular blending component. On the other end of the spectrum, it's often developed into a flagship red, cosseted in lots of wood. Its future is still being written. If you like rich reds, try the Stellenbosch Pinotages; if you prefer more elegant reds, sample those from the Walker Bay.

...Fact...

In King Tutankhamen's Egypt (around 1300 BC), the commoners drank beer and the upper class sipped on wine.

CORPORATES

'Everything counts in large
amounts.'

– Depeche Mode

A healthy industry of any sort has the small guys who take the world on their own terms; the mid-size who expand the varietal diversity and approach; and the big guys who have the clout to stabilise the whole structure. These are the Corporates, where wine is business. For people in the broader wine industry, this attitude is great. The ability to throw some serious moolah behind brands makes wine better known; it takes wine to the people, puts it on the supermarket shelves and in the far-flung towns.

The Corporates get things done, make profits and establish healthy business relationships. Some snooty wine lovers may have a less than excited reaction to them, but don't let this preconception stand in the way of some exploration – there are some great wines at good prices from these wineries. This is because they bring the range and the power to make change to the mix, and this often benefits the consumer.

They have the scope to make wine a product that lives in every price category at good quality – and they usually offer many delightful extras, diversions, and activities on the winelands visit. The Corporates offer you, the consumer, choices, both in price and wine style. There is comfort in consistency, and, if you like your wine not to vary or play any nasty tricks on you, these are the guys to go to. Volume means a great deal more control over the final product and, when it comes to moody, changeable wine, this certainly has a smoothing effect.

If they can be slightly anonymous you have to forgive them on the grounds of value and dependability, for these are the friendly uncles of the wine world. They sometimes try to make themselves hip by throwing some slang around or changing their labels through a carefully debated committee decision with ultimately negligible results; but they're always happy for our attention.

The examples of the Corporates you'll find here bring good wines to the party – they have realised that it's not good enough just to spend advertising money; you have to improve the product. In these times of global competition, you can't move about with an ordinary quiver of wines.

Nederburg Wines

༄

The big daddy of the Corporates, from a philosophical point of view, if not also in terms of scale of production, is Nederburg Wines. This farm began life as another large colonial spread with manor house but none of the owners ever managed to focus the winemaking operations until the arrival of a German immigrant, Johann Graue, who acquired the farm in 1937.

Sonstraal Road,
Daljosafat, Paarl
(021) 877-5132
Mon-Fri 8.30am-5pm,
Sat 10am-2pm, Nov-
Mar also Sun 10am-4pm
Facilities ★ ★ ★
Prices $ to $$

Ahead of his time – or his local contemporaries – he began by replanting the vines extensively with the belief that good wine began in the vineyard. Graue had left a successful brewery business in Germany, so his grasp of fermentation processes was good, and he soon realised that the warmth of the Cape summers was not ideal for white wine production. This insight led to a significant breakthrough – steel tanks that could ferment the grapes at cooler temperatures.

This technological improvement was the beginning of the new Cape white wine industry – and marked the stellar growth of the name Nederburg. The winery began to source grapes from far and wide and created an extensive range based on good vineyard management (along with the establishment of nurseries) and modern cellar practice.

Off these solid foundations, Nederburg has grown monumentally over the years and is now a central part of the liquor giant, Distell. Cellarmaster Günter Brözel joined in 1956 and left only in 1989 after achieving remarkable success with red wines as well as his introduction of dessert wines in the German style: the noble late harvest wines (see page 29). Edelkeur became a brand known internationally, and is available only at the annual Nederburg Auction, started in 1974 as a clearing house for special and aged wines. This auction is now a winelands institution – and a glamorous fashion show. Nothing wrong with a bit of Corporate glitz.

The next era of innovation at this giant began at the turn of the century with the appointment of talented Romanian winemaker Razvan Macici and his young winemaking and marketing team and the revamping of all their (many) labels. The wine and styles have been repackaged to suit modern tastes: away with the leaner, tighter wines and in with fruity, rounder wines.

Today, Nederburg Wines HQ in Paarl features a modern,

interactive tourist centre, where you can travel by glass lift through the process of winemaking and get a closer look at the workings of a modern cellar. A good measure of the farm's winemaking history is also thrown in, in the form of a heritage centre and museum. This is the perfect place for a closer look at the evolution of the modern Cape Corporate.

▲ pick of the wines

They have a three-tier consumer wine range with dozens of wines. 'Manor House' for the fancy stuff (here the Sauvignon Blanc is a winner); 'Winemaster's Reserve' for a selection of fine wines (the pick is Edelrood, a red blend, and the Shiraz); and the 'Foundation' range: wines for casual drinking, these are typically very easy-going. In general, the wines here are seeing considerable improvement and they are already firm restaurant favourites.

while in the area

Do

• The cellar tour with its look into the nitty-gritty of winemaking as well as some historical insights.

Eat

• Call ahead for picnic lunches on the farm in summer 0800-200867.

Flagstone Winery

With seemingly unlimited energy and fresh ideas, Bruce Jack burst on to the Cape wine stage like a dervish. Flagstone was the name he gave to his cellar and wines, and it's a good thing that the name suggests grounding, because it soon became evident that the rest is perpetual motion.

Heartland **AECI**, De Beers Road, Somerset West
(021) 686-8640
Tues-Sun 10am-6pm
Facilities ★★
Prices $$

The wines were originally made in the novel location of Cape Town's V&A Waterfront but the expansion of this as well as his own growing output took Jack to the equally quirky and even more suitable environs of an old dynamite factory near Somerset West where the walls are now adorned with signs that light up with words like 'seduce'.

Here you'll find wine names and labels that obliterate the more traditional and conservative approach that wine is known for – 'Dark Horse Shiraz', 'Writer's Block Pinotage' and 'Dragon Tree' are some of the labels – so with all this individualism it was a surprise to many when the winery was bought by the world's largest wine company, Constellation Wines, a few years ago, making the most idiosyncratic South African wine brand part of a corporate stable that includes the mega-seller Kumala. How the world has changed.

But not the wines, thankfully. The spirit of Flagstone Winery remains rooted in sourcing pockets of unique, expressive grapes in unusual areas of the Cape – like the southern tip of Africa, Agulhas, and the Swartland. These 'imported' grapes travelled to Jack's cellar in big refrigeration containers and experiments in the expression of pure grape essence began. A keen follower of all that's new, Jack absorbs current information and innovates with ease, so the move to screwcap closures for most of their wines was a no-brainer: 'After all the care, how can you leave wine to the risk of a spoilt cork?' In the cellar, the techniques are similarly forward-thinking, with the emphasis on preserving fresh, lively fruit.

Jack studied and worked in California and returned with the desire to make generous wines that people love to drink. He also has a penchant for poetry (exemplified in his creative back label copy), and a conversation with him easily moves from discussions on the science of wine structure to lyrical diversions into the importance of preserving the vital line of life energy from the grape into the bottle ...

The result is a range of wines that are easy to approach, but continually surprise with their individuality. As an example of the modern corporate, this is a great template.

🍾 pick of the wines

The Dark Horse Shiraz demonstrates Jack's way with labels and his mastery of the supple wine style: this baby is full of Shiraz's seductive essence, as is Writer's Block Pinotage, with none of the variety's rusticity. 'Two Roads' is a fantastic white blend and if you're a Sauvignon Blanc fan, try the Fiona. Flagstone wines are all marked by a drinkability that verges on hedonism.

while in the area

Eat

✦ At Alex Garden Restaurant, 10 Van Riebeeck Street off Beach Road (021) 854-6793, or head into Somerset West to Henri's (evenings only), Corner Lourensford and Main Road, Somerset West (021) 852 6442.

Graham Beck Wines

Graham Beck Wines proves that a commercial operation need not be dull. Cellars in both Robertson and Franschhoek give you an idea of the scope of this winery, and the range of wines they produce is bountiful. At the same time, the wineries are each marvels of modern architecture, really bold statements of the new that vividly stand out in the traditional landscape of the Cape winelands. In fact, Graham Beck Franschhoek used to be a traditional winery;

Coastal: R45 outside Franschhoek
(021) 874-1258
Mon-Fri 9am-5pm, Sat 10am-3pm
Facilities ★★
Prices $$ to $$$

Robertson: R60 between Robertson and Worcester
(023) 626-1214
Mon-Fri 9am-5pm, Sat 10am-3pm

it's been morphed into a dramatic new entity with stark lines, colours and the trademark oversized artworks that you'll find at the other Graham Beck properties (which includes Constantia's

Steenberg Winery and Hotel, as well as the Robertson winery).

Graham Beck Robertson has its attention largely focused on creating the Cape's leading sparkling wines, but is also known as the home to some very fine Shiraz (including the famous 'The Ridge'). Robertson turns out to have soils that are eminently suitable to two things that the actual Graham Beck, mining magnate extraordinaire, really loves: horses and bubbly. The secret's in the rich lime deposits in the soil here, good for vine roots and good for strong equine bones. It's no coincidence that another part of the world with such lime-rich soil is Champagne.

The Graham Beck range is led by a collection of 'name' wines: The Joshua, The William, The Andrew – so if you are better at remembering faces you may become a little confused … There is also Coffeestone Cabernet Sauvignon and Lonehill Chardonnay – which at least make their introduction somewhat easier by using the family name. These 'name' wines are serious in intent, followed by another range of varietal wines, and then a collection of friendly blends. It's an extensive selection, but each wine is market-savvy: marvels of craft and quality and marketing. Their end point consumer is well established – and this market well identified. They may even have your telephone number.

Graham Beck Wines is a good example of the melding of Old and New World. They have chosen pockets of vines that deliver excellent quality and which are not necessarily on the proprietary farms themselves – but are scattered across the vast Cape landscape. These carefully sourced grapes go through the sensitive care of modern 'placeless' wineries, and emerge consistent, characteristic and dressed in stylish labels designed to fit certain markets perfectly. That's successful modern wine.

🍾 pick of the wines

The Old Road Pinotage is a unique wine from vineyards planted in 1963. It's rare to taste this heritage in Cape wines. The complete opposite is Pinno, a young 'pop' Pinotage that's great chilled for summer days. The Ridge Syrah is a modern shiraz in the best sense: bold but richly layered. Brut Blanc de Blancs is a beautiful, elegant bubbly; while the Brut Rosé is the sexy sister. Take your pick from the consistent range: the Gamekeeper's Reserve Chenin Blanc is really good too.

while in the area (Franschhoek)

Eat

* At The French Connection, a bistro (on the main street of the town) that serves good comfort food on the corner of Huguenot and Bordeaux streets (021) 876-4056.

Up on high

What the Cape has, which the fancy wine regions of France lack, is sunlight and warmth. Our vineyards don't struggle to ripen grapes. In Europe, their best years are the ones when there was enough sunlight to get fruit ripeness. We have the opposite problem – our vineyards can easily make grapes overripe, too sweet, with a too high potential alcohol (not that that stops many winemakers: hyper-ripe wines with 15-16 per cent alc abound). For this reason, many of the better vineyard sites are higher up to take advantage of the cooler conditions of altitude. A cooler climate helps slower ripening, which in turn means more complexity in the grape flavours.

Other Noteworthy Corporates

Spier

The Spier wine complex is one of the most diverse entertainment zones in the Cape winelands: numerous restaurants, a golf course, lovely grounds and gardens, a hotel, an amphitheatre, a spa, a train – and a wildlife centre with real live cheetahs and eagles. There's also a wine shop

Annandale Road,
Stellenbosch
(021) 809-1143
Mon-Sun 9am-5pm
Facilities ★ ★ ★
Prices $ to $$

if you don't feel like driving anywhere else (and another Spier shop at Sun City if you are in that neck of the woods) so here the usual reason to visit a wine farm has been turned on its head: you're as likely to come for the wine as to bring the kids to look at animals and cavort in a colourful play park, have a light lunch alfresco or dine in the African extravaganza restaurant. This place has panache. (Cheetahs sure help.)

Yet, for all the international wine tourism that this 'winelands resort' represents, there's a great deal of history here. It's one of the oldest farms in the area, and was once farmed by Cecil John Rhodes (see Boschendal, page 23). The original buildings are all still to be seen in the mix of commerciality, making a stroll around the grounds an interesting and rewarding fusion of the old and the very new.

If you were imagining that the wines would be rather anonymous (for which you would be forgiven), you will be happily surprised to find wines that have a great deal of charm and no shortage of quality. There are multiple tiers of them, carefully tuned to deliver the right quality at the appropriate volume, packaged in approachable livery.

◗ pick of the wines

The Private Collection Sauvignon Blanc and Chenin Blanc are show-stoppers, powerful in flavour and full of developed, bouncy fruit flavours. Of the reds, the Private Collection Cabernet Sauvignon is the muscular pick, but you also have to try the wines in the 'Vintage Selection' range, particularly the Malbec-Cabernet Franc-Petit Verdot.

Perdeberg Winery

Literally 'horse mountain' but more specifically a reference to the herds of zebra that roamed the hills here where the farms, now members of this co-operative style winery, are situated. In the spirit of many early twentieth century Cape wine regions, wine farmers in the Perdeberg were

Off R302 (off N1)
towards Malmesbury
(021) 869-8244
Mon-Fri 8am-5pm, Sat
and holidays 10am-2pm
Facilities ★
Prices $ to $$

unhappy with the low prices they were getting for their produce, and in 1942 they set up their own co-operative winery to beneficiate their raw product, the grape.

They managed without a formal winemaker until 1956 and from here there was a concerted drive to modernisation in their winemaking. For example, Perdeberg was the second winery in South Africa to use cold fermentation (see Nederburg Wines, page 50) and along with other new technologies from Europe this farmers' co-operative has now grown into a strong corporate built on the 46 member farms, many of whom are third generation producers for Perdeberg. They've successfully made the transition from farmers' collective to Corporate.

But that's not enough to make them special (South Africa has a number of former co-operatives, now companies). It's the terrain they are working in and the age of the vines. The Perdeberg is both a historic wine region and at the same time very *du jour*. In one of those quirks of history, many of the vines planted here are now of great age (in the Cape that's 50+ years) because back in the day the small, mixed agriculture farmers planted white varieties for distillation rebates and it so

happened that these farmers never pulled these old vines out –
while the rest of the Cape's vineyards were rapidly replanted in
the commercialisation of the 1990s. The combination of rare
old vine stock and the Perdeberg's naturally granitic soils has
resulted in an area of undeniable excitement.

pick of the wines

Perdeberg Winery's range offers great value, even before you
fill your boot with their value for money wines. As an area that
is famous for Chenin Blanc, you should try their standard label
Chenin Blanc, as well as their fancy and luscious Rex Equus
Chenin Blanc. On the reds, the Pinotage delivers pure fruit and
flavour, again as budget wine or in the luxury (though still well-
priced) guise.

KWV

If you don't live in South Africa,
it's highly likely that the very first
Cape wine you came across was a
bottle of KWV. The 'Ko-operatieve
Wijnbouwers Vereniging van Zuid-
Afrika Beperkt' is *the* historic
monolith of the Cape wine industry
– formed in the early part of the

Kohler Street, Paarl
(021) 807-3008
Mon-Sat 9am-4.30pm
Tours: Mon-Sat 10am,
10.30am, 2.15pm and
10.15am (German)

twentieth century to protect the wine growers' prices in the face
of a terrible slump. It grew into a powerful body that regulated
the industry, specifically the export market, for decades. Along

the way it also became a wine brand in its own right, and a strong one at that, with presence in 35 international markets. For this reason, most KWV wines are arguably better known overseas than at home.

In recent post-apartheid years, and with South Africa's re-entry into the open market, KWV has had to endure the incursion of other local Corporates with aspirations of world domination, so it no longer enjoys an open playing field, but it remains a powerful wine brand – and one of the leading brandy manufacturers in the world. As wineries go, they make no bones about their Corporate manner – as a visit to their website complete with their current share price and company news will tell you.

The traditional home of the KWV is in Paarl at the fabulously historic La Concorde house, but for the winelands visitor their 'emporium' in nearby Kohler Street is home to daily guided tours in English and German that describe the history of the KWV, and the broader Cape winelands. You can also taste and buy the wines here, including the well-loved 'Roodeberg', which is probably their most famous label.

♗ pick of the wines

KWV make a couple of ranges of wine, the easy-drinking Pearly Bay, Laborie, Cathedral Cellars, Roodeberg and the eponymous KWV range. They also make the mocha-flavoured Café Culture red for lovers of wine that tastes more of coffee and chocolate. Look out for the KWV Reserve Cabernet Sauvignon and Shiraz, while the KWV 10-year old brandy is brilliant and sells at an excellent price.

FUTURISTS

'Neither do men put new wine
into old bottles'

– Matthew 9:17

With a canny eye on global trends and an innovative approach, the Futurists are ever ready to tackle something new. It's not that they're necessarily the new kids on the block, but they're the guys who are constantly willing to change the way it's always been done. The Futurists will be the first to have The Latest Toy, or New Theory. If it's fashionable, they're interested, but the chief motivation is being innovative.

They have progressive ways with wine and a dynamic approach. The Futurists are also the most likely to have experimental batches in the cellar, to plant new varieties and to design fresh labels. They want to combine the best of what's come before with something that's never been done before. Fusion. Experimentation. Alchemy.

Many of them will have worked in or taken inspiration from other New World wineries; they are well travelled and have an anything-is-possible attitude.

Tradition is certainly not discarded, but it is given a serious once-over. The Futurists question the old rules and are always ready to create some nascent traditions of their own. Their cellars are also likely to express this futurism, with innovative architecture; while the vineyards that they source from may well be far flung and varied: not for them the old conventions of grapes only from the estate.

The winemaker or owner is a celebrated and public figure here, often a feisty, opinionated individual. If he isn't, then the marketing team is about to arrive. In the mix, the Futurists deftly handle marketing; in fact it is one of their greatest allies, for marketing and advertising love the tang of the new. A fresh angle makes for good copy and sexy bottles that stand out on the overtraded supermarket shelves. A couple of publicity stunts are certainly not amiss. Modernity likes the unusual; it trades on the point of difference.

Fairview

꧁

One of the Cape's pre-eminent movers and shakers is Charles Back of Fairview. This is a family farm that had steadily been making good wine since the mid-1970s, was then taken by the scruff, energetically spring-cleaned and turned into a wine phenomenon. Super-charging the brand, Back made waves that were felt as far away as the Rhône in France, where his cheekily named wines took a dig at famous French names in wordplay like 'Goats do Roam'. Gallic noses twitched indignantly.

Suid-Agter Paarl Road, Paarl
(021) 863-2450
Mon-Fri 8.30am-5pm,
Sat 8.30am-1pm
Facilities ★ ★ ★
Prices $$$

This farm does have a goat fetish. The on-site restaurant's name is the Goatshed and their latest wine range is called La Capra. To explain, it has to be said that Charles Back has had the help of a few enterprising goats. Vetting visitors to the farm from their goat tower, they have also been responsible for the goat's cheese for which Fairview is well known – a separate business that has now grown to include a wide range of internationally acclaimed goat's and cow's milk cheeses.

But that was just the start. Roaming through the vineyards and selecting the best grapes to eat, the goats suggested the name Goats do Roam and later Goat Roti (Côte Roti), and these innovative wines became hugely successful. The grapes harnessed in these wines are similar to the French originals; they're styled on the robust and juicy varieties like Shiraz, Grenache, Carignan, Viognier and Crouchen, amongst others – some exotic fruit to our shores, but eminently suitable because of our climatic similarities to southern Europe.

The restless Back wanted more. In 1997, a satellite winery established in the Swartland, called Spice Route, produced its first wines. These full-flavoured reds had the judges and wine commentators reaching for their stars. Taking further lessons from the goats' free roaming style, Fairview has shaken free from the options that the traditional wine areas in the Cape offer, and has ranged into unusual and novel areas to find good vineyard land. This Fairview sense of experimentation has resulted in single vineyard wines with names like Pegleg Carignan, Solitude Shiraz and Akkerbos Chardonnay – names that celebrate the provenance of the grapes and their sense of uniqueness. They come from here, there and everywhere, and they constantly surprise the establishment.

Where will 'The Goatfather' roam next? Charles Back is a ground-breaker, opening up new terrain and setting trends in his search for unique wines. In the meanwhile, the tasting room is one of the friendliest and best organised in the Cape.

🍾 pick of the wines

Goats do Roam in Villages White is citric, fresh and delicious drinking. Fairview Shiraz is warm and earthy in a full modern style, but this Shiraz specialist also has the fantastic Cyril Back Shiraz and luscious Solitude Shiraz. A Grenache-dominated wine of immense character is Caldera, as is the Oom Pagel Sémillon.

while in the area

Do

* Buy some wonderful cheeses – a small tasting fee allows wine and cheese sampling.

Eat

* At the Goatshed on the farm itself, where good bread and tasty food are on offer.
* Head into Paarl to eat at Marc's where the Mediterranean food is full of flavour. 129 Main Road (021) 863-3980; or Terra Mare, for great Italian food, 90 Main Road (021) 863-4805.

Tokara

You'll find this marvellous piece of modern architecture at the summit of the stunning Helshoogte Pass between Stellenbosch and Franschhoek: a bold rampart

Helshoogte Pass
(021) 808-5900
Mon-Fri 10am-5pm

that juts out from the hillside and hangs defiantly over the vale of vineyards beneath it, with a high-end restaurant featuring floating decks to make the most of the awesome position.

On the left-hand side rows of stainless steel tanks shine behind very designer glass walls, and the winery and tasting room are bedecked with works of very contemporary and quite clearly expensive art. For this is the winery of banking mogul G T Ferreira, and its confident modernity rocked the Cape on its arrival at the turn of the century. And then, to everyone's surprise, instead of unleashing an array of expensive wines into the market, they waited. And waited. They were waiting for the quality of the wine to reach their expectations. Here, the expectation is to be world-class. Of course, the highest quality is not a modern concept by any means, but it takes bags of confidence to stare the market down until you think you are approaching this level, and it takes no shortage of that chimerical thing called 'cash flow'.

In this light, Tokara is the leading example of a modern and fast-growing collection of Cape wineries – those that are bank-rolled by wealthy individuals who are quite willing to do what is right by the wine, and who, while they respect the market, are not ruled by it. So Tokara has meticulously groomed vineyards that benefit from infra-red photography to tell them how the vines are feeling; it has a gravity-assisted cellar and a wine press that uses an inert environment for minimal gaseous interference ... name the modern winemaking toy and you'll likely find it here. In fact, winemaker Miles Mossop is in control of his winery through a computerised interface, and small, humanoid robots make the wine. Well, not yet. In so many ways, winemaking remains a hands-on job.

However they do it, it works. As mentioned, for the first few years, Tokara only released what is now the second label, Zondernaam ('without name'); now these are complemented by the Tokara range of classic varietal wines and their flagships: a blended white and red. There is fantastic quality in both, since both are made with the same meticulous care. They're modern wines in the sense that they're plush, polished and seamlessly made. They embody the international character of modernity perfectly.

♦ pick of the wines

Tokara White is a simply superb blend, class and elegance personified – as is the Tokara Red, a very classic Bordeaux-style blend. The Zondernaan Cabernet Sauvignon is a winner, as is the Zondernaan Sauvignon Blanc – in general the Zondernaam wines over-deliver on quality for the price.

while in the area

Do

- Buy their superb olive oil. They have nearly 20 hectares of their highest lands planted to olives and the oil is really good.

Eat

- ◆ At one of the restaurants on the estate, which specialises in innovation and the fabulous views that are on offer.

Solms-Delta

Sometimes the key to modernity lies in the past. It certainly does at Solms-Delta, a relatively new winery that released its first wines in 2004. Here, a return to very traditional winemaking alongside a respectful representation of Cape history is the cornerstone of their success.

Off R45 on the
Simondium side of
Franschhoek valley
(021) 874 3937
Daily 9am-5pm

Mark Solms is a neuroscientist extraordinaire. This has to rate pretty much as high as rocket scientist, and it may explain why no one else has really presented a Cape wine farm and wines in this manner before. Realising that the land that the wine farm was situated on held a history that was millennia old, Solms excavated and explored as he built the winery. The result of the fieldwork and research is a fantastic cultural museum and active archaeological sites that you can visit, in addition to tasting the fascinating wines or lunching at the restaurant that specialises in, again, modern traditional cuisine. The museum tells the story of the land through the voices of those that have gone before, adding a riveting emotional component to a place that could so easily have been 'another' beautiful Cape winery.

Modern winemaking is generally grounded on optimal ripeness in the vineyard and it's an approach to winemaking that focuses on hygiene, minimal intervention and new oak barrels. These tenets have become gospel, but for Solms there was an opportunity to be innovative by going back to a technique in winemaking that was last used in ancient times: the desiccation of grapes, more bluntly known as 'strangulation'.

This approach was championed thousands of years ago by the ancient Greeks and Romans (when corporal punishment was less frowned upon) as a way to intensify flavour and colour while retaining fresh acidity – a component that is like gold in South Africa's warm climate. Thought Solms: If this used to work in the warm areas of the Med – why not in warm Franschhoek? Work it did: the result is wines of unusual complexity and depth, while retaining freshness.

Another, very modern, task for the Cape wine farm is the redress of the inequalities of the South African past. Here, a trust was established to represent the tenant-workers on the estate, which trust purchased a neighbouring property which contributes to the grape production, making the workers partners in the wine business. And more: a centre for the preservation of Cape colloquial music has been established, and there is likely to be no end to the innovation that Solms-Delta embodies. If the new can often look like change simply for the sake of change, here's a living example of creative change that brings forth dynamic and useful novelty.

🍾 pick of the wines

'Hiervandaan' is a Shiraz-led blend of lovely weight and rich flavour; while the 'Lekkerwijn' rosé is one of the Cape's best examples. 'Langarm' is a delicious red blend featuring Pinotage and Touriga, Tannat, et al. If you are keen on decadently rich wines, the 'Africana' and 'Koloni' are made in full desiccation style for intensity and weight.

while in the area

Do

♦ Take the time to absorb some of the info in the museum and see the digs, open same times as the tasting room. Ideally set aside a morning, then have lunch.

Eat

♦ At the restaurant on the estate, Fyndraai, which specialises in real Cape cuisine and has lovely views of the mountains and vineyards.

...Fact...

South Africa's total vineyard plantings, at approximately 103 000 hectares, is more or less the same as just one of France's wine regions, Bordeaux.

Other
Noteworthy
Futurists

Warwick Estate

꙳

It's been over two decades since Norma and Stan Ratcliffe first made some red wine on the back of a bakkie to launch the family label Warwick and a great deal has changed since then, but not the trademark enthusiasm that initiated the brand. This continues with energetic son Mike at the helm of a now very successful international business.

R44 Between Klapmuts and Stellenbosch
(021) 884-3146
Mon-Fri 10am-5pm, Sat 10am-4pm, Sun Oct-Apr 10am-4pm
Facilities ★ ★ ★
Prices $$

Along the way Norma also cleared a path for female winemakers with her outspoken talents and energy. In celebration of this strong role that women play in the wine world, Warwick Estate adopted the female figurine of the 'Marriage Cup' as the Warwick symbol, and now the unpretentious tasting room has a collection of them on display. It may now seem normal, but female winemakers in this androcentric world are a pretty novel thing.

The placid environment of the farm belies the estate's highly innovative winemaking that includes partnerships with high-flying international consultants like America's Phil Freese and high-tech farming that employs 'mesoclimatic temperature sensors to collect vineyard data at frequent intervals for micromanipulation of the vineyards' ... you get the picture.

And modernity continues in Warwick's confident relations with publicity. They certainly understand the importance of a high profile – witness their wines being served to presidents and kings ... and a favourite of the punters in Vegas, where top hotels list their wines.

pick of the wines

The Trilogy has attracted awards and praise, all well-founded because the wine has a great track record with the critics and the public; a big, plush, but serious wine. The Three Cape Ladies used to refer to the trinity of Cab, Merlot and Pinotage, now there is actually a fourth – Shiraz – in there, and it's a good wine. A more recent addition to the range is The First Lady, a medium-bodied Cabernet/Merlot blend to commemorate Norma's achievements.

Ken Forrester Wines

If there were a governmental position for an international South African wine ambassador, Ken Forrester would be a front-runner. Since the mid 1990s, he's been roaming the globe, drumming up support for his wines, South African wines and Chenin Blanc with

Winery Road, off R44
between Somerset West
and Stellenbosch
(021) 855-2374
Mon-Fri 9am-5pm, Sat
10.30am-1.30pm
Facilities ★
Prices $ to $$$

seemingly limitless reserves of energy. In many respects, this is a Big Hitter, but there's the restless energy of an iconoclast around Forrester.

Take the subject of corks. He gets quite animated when describing how these ruin too many good bottles of wine due to their propensity for TCA spoilage (which is what makes a wine 'corked'). So he is moving steadily towards screwcaps on all his wines, from the easy-drinkers to the top of the range. While most wineries are waiting for the rest of the industry to do it, he is doing it. That's the Futurist spirit.

Take Chenin Blanc, the 'Cinderella' grape, so called because it's the pretty girl who never really gets the man, the wallflower. Forrester hasn't just made a Chenin and doesn't just sing its praises in the midst of the others in the portfolio, he's made a full range of them, and he even made his flagship wine a Chenin (the FMC) – and then put a bold price tag on it. His Cinderellas are hitting the ballroom floor.

🍾 pick of the wines

One of the most striking wines in the Cape is the FMC Chenin Blanc, made from old bushvine grapes; it's a remarkably rich and complex wine that's packed with quality fruit and endlessly layered. His Ken Forrester Chenin Blanc is another great wine in a less voluptuous style, but still no flimsy waif. And on the reds, the Gypsy is a delicious Shiraz and Grenache blend of great flair, and also try the Merlot.

Jordan Wine Estate

It's all about family at this modern winery where the so-called 'retired' dad captains the harvester and husband and wife Gary and Cathy Jordan take care of the vineyards and wines. But this is no chilled home on the range. Since training in winemaking at UC Davis in California, this duo has poured constant energy linked to a dynamic

Stellenbosch Kloof Road, Vlottenberg
(021) 881-3441
Mon-Fri 10am-4.30, Sat (Nov-April) 9.30am-2.30pm, Sat closes 12.30pm at other times of year
Facilities ★★★
Prices $$

aptitude for development into the family spread. The strong thread of a cross-disciplinary approach stems from their science and numbers background – Gary a former geologist and Cathy an economist.

Jordan is one Cape winery that defines contemporary winemaking. The solid range of wines has a real polish to it: they carry an accomplished air. This has been refined and taken to a peak in the Cobbler's Hill Bordeaux-style blend and the 'Nine Yards' Chardonnay Reserve where the best of their barrels are bottled. The first of the two names refers to the father's house on the hill and the family business, Jordan shoes; and the second to the lengths that they went to in making the wine.

Well worth a visit for the views and the new restaurant, the farm is beautifully situated in the Stellenboschkloof hills; on some slopes the panorama includes both oceans. This means they have a wonderful variety of aspects for vines and this natural boon, coupled with Gary's soil science, has been a magic partnership. Awards for their modern wines, soft and full of flavour, have poured in, and the winery has grown quickly, and where the family is gracious and restrained, the wines are graceful and bold.

pick of the wines

Cobbler's Hill is a masterpiece of seamless, pure flavour: a beautifully balanced wine in a full, rich style. Their Chardonnay also carries the beauty of balance: powerful but not clumsy. Their way with wood is well represented in the Blanc Fumé, an oaked Sauvignon Blanc that's good with food.

INDIVIDUALISTS

'To live is like to love – all
reason is against it and all
healthy instinct for it.'

– Samuel Butler

There are those who obey only their own rules – the mavericks and non-conformists – often they are eccentric, sometimes out-and-out rebellious. They hold risk close, like a dear friend, and sail gladly into headwinds. In the wheel of the wine universe, they are the opposite of the Corporates. Nor are they Stylists, because the projection of image is secondary to them; they just can't help themselves from doing it their way.

Many of them are happiest to run intimate operations, where they do pretty much everything themselves in order to keep their personal vision pure. It goes with the territory that these wineries are based solidly on the personality of the winemaker.

They are likely to be found in unusual and far-flung places, on the outskirts and on the frontiers, finding pockets of vineyard that are remote, unexplored and full of potential. The Individualists like to unlock, tease out and express the vines, so potentiality is the stuff that excites them. Individualists are the ultimate terroir-ists, believing that the expression of the land is a near holy calling. Near? It won't take much pressure for them to speak in spiritual terms of the soil and plants they nurture so carefully.

When it comes to making the wine, they are likely to be

Luddites, forsaking the comfort of convention for the lore of the ancient and time honoured. Working in intimate cellars and with a hands-on approach, they treat the wines as precious individuals, allowing the expression of what will naturally come from the grapes, using wild yeasts, gravity, no filtration and even phases of the moon to play their part.

Some of them are refugees from the mainstream, escapees from industry who have stumbled upon another way, a more poetic path. Others have never done it any other way, starting to make wine in garages, sheds and industrial fridges. Some are still tiny operations, while others have grown, though the maverick ethos gives them all a darkstar focused gravity. These are men of the earth, always closer to the soil and the vine than the cellar. They never had to learn that good wines start in the vines; instinct took care of that.

Springfield Estate

In a world with far too much product and not enough personality, the wines of Springfield stand out without ever being stand-offish. The Bruwer family has been farming in the Robertson valley for many generations; with vines for the last three. This rootedness has given

R317 (Bonnievale Rd) just outside Robertson
(023) 626-3661
Mon-Fri 8am-5pm, Sat 9am-4pm
Facilities ★
Price $$

brother and sister Abrie and Jeanette Bruwer a pragmatic, tried and tested knowledge, and this, along with a penchant for the grand gesture and a poetic approach to winemaking, has swept them from conformity.

They will tell you that all starts in the vineyards, and Abrie has learnt over time to manage the particularities of his warm Robertson climate and their mineral-rich soils and fused this with his underlying philosophy that is rooted in his saying that 'you mustn't do what's right for you, but what's right for the wine', and a belief that, if nature does it, it's probably best. So his vineyards are combed by a voracious army of geese that move like stumpy ghosts through the vines, gobbling up all the snails and other molesters. This example may seem picturesque and quaint, yet it contains the seeds of rebellion – chemical intervention, the norm, has been forsaken.

The irony is that non-conformity begins with a healthy respect for tradition. Trellising the vines in ancient French formations, very close together for competitiveness, Bruwer later uses natural yeasts to ferment most of his musts (see page 84) – a risky, drawn-out proposition that results in more failed fermentations than most winemakers would be courageous enough to face – sometimes resulting in big tanks of premium wine vinegar. His cellar works without pumps for gentler handling of the grapes. Then he leaves his premium red wines to lie for two years in the barrel and another two in the bottle to release them only 'when they say they are ready'. That's a lot of capital investment deciding to be ready.

This insouciance to the pressures of cash flow is not achieved without sacrifice. Abrie Bruwer's opinion about the potential revenue that he is effectively putting under his mattress? 'I'd rather have the money here, where I can keep a proper eye on it, than give it to someone else to look after.' That's the Individualist spirit.

As you may gather, the Springfield Bruwers have also mastered that other French tradition – romance – and tell beautiful stories about their wines, giving them poetic names like 'Life from Stone' and 'Work of Time'. The Sauvignon Blancs from this winery continually attract headlines – as striking and egregious as they are. But all the wines are marked by poise, refinement and a heady, seductive drinkability, even in their infancy. The wry Bruwer bases it on a simple human observation: 'A young wine that's no good doesn't mature into a good one. I mean do you go and start dating someone ugly hoping they'll turn out all right in the end?'

pick of the wines

If you can find a more interesting Sauvignon Blanc than Life from Stone – a blazingly fresh, mineral wine – you're doing well. On the other end of the textural spectrum, Wild Yeast Chardonnay is soft and peachy and utterly charming. Of the reds, how to choose? They are all remarkable for their gentle tannins and purity of fruit. Okay, go for the Méthode Ancienne Cabernet Sauvignon – the name that also sums up the estate.

while in the area

Eat

* Reuben's at The Robertson Small Hotel (023) 626-7200 or email reservations@ therobertsonsmallhotel.com.

Wild yeasts

Wine is the product of the fermentation of grape juice. The sugars in the grape are converted to alcohol by yeasts – the engines of winemaking. Wild yeasts are pretty much as the name suggests: not the cultivated ones, but the yeasts that occur naturally in the environment. Cultivated yeasts have been selected and developed in labs to accentuate certain characteristics. Working with wild ones adds an X-factor and complexity, but you never know when they are going to down tools and strike – an alarming development that can cause fermentation to fail. Inoculated yeasts, on the other hand, are engineered to go like the Energizer bunny and not give in until the job's done.

Sadie Family Wines

What do you do if you are working in a successful cellar and have made a wine that's universally hailed as one of the world's best Shirazes … but there's a nagging voice inside you that says you can do better if

R317 (Bonnievale Rd) just outside Robertson
(023) 626-3661
Mon-Fri 8am-5pm, Sat 9am-4pm
Facilities ★
Price $$

only you could do it completely your way? Well, you sell your car to buy a few barrels, borrow some space and money and go for it. That's if you're Eben Sadie, with strong nerves but an even stronger vision and boundless desire to go all the way.

A few years later, and Sadie Family Wines is internationally recognised as making some of South Africa's finest wines, and Sadie is still doing it his way. They're based in the Swartland, an area that's never been fashionable but is now the centre of ever-growing attention, thanks in no small measure to his remarkable reds. It's here, in a tiny, hand-built winery, that Sadie exerts every mitochondrion to the creation of wines that carry unmistakable individuality.

Spending lavishly on the best bottles and the best corks for the most perfect seal ('these are areas out of my control, so I buy the best') is the culmination of abundant personal attention to every other detail – with the area of the most attention being the vineyard. The preferred vineyards in his case are extreme – or, to put it another way, as unadulterated and natural as possible – far-flung, high up in inaccessible vales, planted traditionally, without trellising and smack in amongst other vegetation for a competitive environment.

Sadie's primary philosophy of winemaking is: 'Create the site, then let the site work for you, not the other way around. Too many winemakers work for the site!' Like many of his outspokenly iconoclastic statements, this rails against all the commercial wines that are made against nature, not in accord with it. Another saying: 'If you aren't brought up with manners you can't just go out and get some.' So too with the essential building blocks of good wine – good grapes, with decent fruit flavours, tannins and acidity (see page 10).

Some may regard the cellar as 'merely' a place where good grapes are guided into the bottle, but his attention here is just as intense, informed by an artisanal and rather antique approach, including the use of concrete 'eggs' to mature the wine. When the grapes arrive at the cellar, a team of 30-plus women sort not just every bunch of grapes, but every berry, with him. It is only at the bottling line where he concedes that technology makes significant additions to quality.

In the cellars of the Swartland and Spain's Priorat (where he makes his highly personal wines for the other half of the year) no pumps are used, no filters, never any added acidity; these short cuts are replaced by personal attention. The intimacy with which Sadie speaks of his wines is the result, and very fine wines they are.

pick of the wines

Columella is a Shiraz-based red blend of great refinement and power. Its deep structure comes from beautifully elaborated tannins and acids. Palladius is a white blend with more depth than most red wines, and a whole lot of charm on top. The Roman, Columella, defined Sadie's approach: 'The most excellent wine is one which has given pleasure by its own natural qualities; nothing must be mixed with it which might obscure the natural taste.'

while in the area

Eat

◆ Bar Bar Black Sheep, Short Street,
  Riebeeck Kasteel
  (022) 448 1031

Boekenhoutskloof Winery

Here's an Individualist winery with something of a split personality. On the one hand making premium wines under the eponymous label, on the other making easy-drinkers called Porcupine Ridge. And then there are the wines in between like The Chocolate Block and The Wolftrap – renegades with lives of their own.

Excelsior Road,
Franschhoek
(021) 876-3320
Mon-Fri 9am-5pm
Facilities ★ ★
Prices $ to $$

Up this part of the Franschhoek valley, the properties are grand. Boekenhoutskloof Winery was founded by an über team of Stylists, some the owners of a leading advertising agency, another of a savvy wine company. The cellar was built in a discreet fashion, and the scene was set for a future as a scrupulous designer winery. And it could have remained 'just' that – except for the restless spirit of the winemaker Marc Kent, who's a congenital maverick.

The winery burst on to the scene in the latter 1990s with reds, notably a Syrah, made in small quantities with the purity of vision of a true Individualist. This wine staggered international judging palates and resulted in a slew of hyperbole, somewhat alarmingly for Kent, who doesn't buy into the hype-machine. It's all about the wine for him, not the reputation. 'Forget the talk, show me the gear' could be his mantra, along with 'the quality of our wines lies in the second half of the bottle'.

The spirit of the Individualist is expressed in their distinctive range of reds, but also strikingly in their one white, a Sémillon. Rhetorically asking why they should make another Chardonnay with the plethora of these on the shelves, Kent turned to his backyard, Franschhoek, which is the traditional home of Sémillon. Access to lovely old and developed bushvines meant a wine of distinction and character, not 'just' another fine Chardonnay. The Individualists' articulation, therefore, of an idea, a philosophy, not just the mechanical reproduction of what is commercially current. Crafted to express texture before fruit flavours, these wines are also an extension of Kent's love for food, and the natural, and ancient, role that wine plays on the table.

Yet these wines, so meticulously made, are now less than 10 per cent of Kent's output. He's taken the same philosophy, of generous wines that express individual character, and applied it to the Porcupine Ridge range, where over-delivery for the price is his benchmark. With bubbling energy, Kent and crew jumped in where they saw good grapes. Measured by growth, the results are spectacular, but what's more interesting is Kent's unbounded love for these wines – if they are more ordinary than the Boekenhoutskloof, it's only in their more blue-collared pricing. It's part of Kent's obvious democratic streak – he doesn't like a snob, nor does he like profiteering wineries that overcharge with no track record. He's a free thinker without pretence, perennially dressed in surf shirts and slops, but with 'gear' to spare.

pick of the wines

Class and elegance are written all over the Cabernet Sauvignon and Syrah, along with the generosity of spirit that Kent strives for – these are not austere wines, but they can go the distance. The Sémillon is a wine apart from any other Cape expression: made in barrel in the old style, it puts fruit second to texture and likes a few years in bottle. The Chocolate Block is a densely flavoured hedonistic wine made up of quite a number of red varieties (but with no added chocolate); and, while all the Porcupine Ridge wines offer great value, it is the Syrah that steals the show.

while in the area

Do

♦ Visit the Huguenot Museum for a history lesson on the French families that founded the town.

Eat

♦ Le Quartier Français for beautiful, modern and award-winning cuisine. 16 Huguenot Road (021) 876-2151.
♦ Reuben's on Huguenot Road for innovative food and a great wine list (021) 876-3772.

Other Noteworthy Individualists

Cederberg Private Cellar

You've heard of far-flung wineries, but when you make wine in a remote mountain valley that's an hour's drive from the nearest small town that's two hours from anywhere, you certainly qualify as an Individualist. But this doesn't mean you make good wine. The fact that the Cederberg vineyards also happen to

N2 north, take Algeria turn-off after Citrusdal and turn right at Algeria, keep driving
(027) 482-2827
Mon-Sat 8am-12, 2pm-4pm, public hols 9am-12
Facilities ★ ★ ★
Prices $$

be the highest in the country and that these grapes are skilfully interpreted is a totally different proposition. Now you have quality wines that are soaked in personality.

David Nieuwoudt's family has been farming this distant part of the world for five generations, so if they're isolated now they were positively on Mars before. They pretty much had to grow all they needed for survival. Thankfully, they decided that wine was one of the necessities to life, and now they grow enough to share it around.

Back in the day, the Nieuwoudts may not have been aware of the awesome advantage their altitude gave them in the quest for quality. Today, David certainly does. South Africa is a natively warm climate, which suits many varieties but can mean it gets too warm for others. Altitude is your ally, cooling your vineyards. New, even higher, vineyards are being established by the team here, a mountainous labour that's certainly no picnic.

Picnics for the rest of us are, however, a great option on this beautiful farm. They have guest cottages on the river, with superb walking and biking trails that penetrate the incredible rock formations this area was famous for long before the wines that are now gathering multiple international awards.

pick of the wines

The five generations are celebrated in a fantastic Cabernet Sauvignon and a Chenin Blanc, while the cellar's Sauvignon Blanc and Shiraz are show-stoppers. At a softer price is the lovely Cederberger, a fruity red blend.

Cape Point Vineyards

As 'terroir' goes, vines stuck between the icy Atlantic seaboard and the windy False Bay on a narrow peninsula is clearly pretty unique. Just as altitude is a powerful vector in determining grape quality in the Cape, so is the exposure to wind – and these Cape Point sites don't

Silvermine Road off
M64, Noordhoek
(021) 785-7660
Visits by appointment
Facilities ★
Prices $$

have wind in the sense that you and I appreciate wind. They have wind in the sense that mad German kite-surfers appreciate wind.

This cellar released its first wine in 2000, and the excited critical acclaim has yet to die down. Luckily, owner Sybrand van der Spuy and Duncan Savage take it in their stride, as is the habit of true individualists. It's not really about plaudits, after all, but the pursuit of great wine.

Savage has proven to have a real feel for Sauvignon Blanc and Sémillon, though he is quick to attribute everything to the fantastic vineyards – as this word attached to the name of their business attests, the vineyard really is the heart of the matter. Modestly, all he claims to do is 'guide the wine into the bottle', but we all know our guidance would not be as good.

As a true Individualist, Savage (with a name like this, he could be no other) actually explores the outer reaches of current wine thinking, experimentally making some of his white wines in ancient clay amphorae – in this way going all out to eschew the 'convention' of wine made in French oak and to hunt for the truly distinctive and original personality of his wines. You can be sure that much excitement is yet to come from this winery.

🍾 pick of the wines

These are possibly the most piercingly pure Sauvignon Blancs and Sémillons in the Cape. If you love classically styled wine, this is your choice. All about intensity matched to refinement, these wines will age well and drink beautifully with food. The white blend, called Isliedh, is magnificent.

Beaumont Wines

Coming down the Houwhoek Pass, most people flash past the quaint town of Bot River, but it's worth a detour if you're a lover of idiosyncratic wineries and bucolic scenery, for this is the home of Beaumont Wines on the Compagnes Drift Farm – established as an old

Off N2 at Bot River, turn left
(028) 284-9194
Mon-Fri 8.30am-5pm,
Sat 10am-3pm
Facilities ★ ★
Prices $ to $$

Dutch East India Company refuelling station in the eighteenth century. Besides the captivatingly rustic winery, this farm is home to one of the oldest watermills in the Cape, now working again after a careful restoration, while the adjacent original mill house and school are currently guest houses (and great for a weekend away).

The farm was derelict in the early 1970s when Jayne and Raoul Beaumont acquired it, and since then the family have gradually re-established its centuries-old wine tradition, making highly individualistic wines from parcels of older vines in the charismatic cellar that still utilises old tech like concrete fermentation tanks and is pretty much the opposite of the slick 'button-and-screen' wineries of the modern Cape – hell, they even still make their port by foot-treading the grapes! As a sign at the winery proclaims: 'Science is no substitute for passion'.

Mother Jayne made the first wines here, and then burly Niels Verburg (now owner of neighbouring Luddite Wines) took over. The winery established its reputation on great Chenin Blanc, Pinotage and the unusual-for-Cape variety, Mourvèdre (native to southern Europe, now increasingly popular here). Today son

Sebastian is the cellar master, and he continues to refine the range to focus on their delightful wooded Chenin and range of earthy blended reds. All the while Bot River is moving into the limelight as an up-and-coming ward on the Cape wine map, and an ever-growing number of wineries is springing up to make use of its unique maritime climate and clay-rich soils. That turn-off may soon be far better known.

pick of the wines

The Hope Marguerite is a fantastic wood fermented and barrel matured Chenin Blanc from old vines – elegant, complex and fresh. Their regular Chenin Blanc is also lovely, fruity and bright; while on the reds, the Pinotage is one of the Cape's most refined, more like Pinot Noir in texture. The Mourvèdre is a full-blooded example of this earthy, 'animale' wine.

...Fact...

Cork was first used in the late seventeenth century, allowing bottles to be laid down. Bottle shapes slowly changed from bulbous to tall and slender as a result.

STYLISTS

'Style is life! It is the very life-
blood of thought!'

– Flaubert

Meet the Stylists of wine, those for whom form is a cornerstone of their approach to winemaking. They want to make good wine, but not just good wine – wine with undeniable panache. Theirs is not wine that wears chinos and golfing shirts. They have established a look that is theirs alone; they're unlikely to be confused with any other. For Stylists, wine is a form of art.

Some are outspoken and opinionated; more are quietly confident. They set trends because of their sophistication, charisma and confidence. They exude cool, focus and belief, and that's why most people are impressed – everyone respects confidence. The wines may be expressive, but never loud and never gauche.

Money also garners respect, and the money behind these wineries is not trifling; for while it may be true that you can't buy style, it sure looks like the upkeep is high once you have it. Stylists are likely to be found in blue-chip vineyards and working with famous varieties, especially attracted to those that reward flair. Pinot Noir is a favourite red, with its artistic reputation and the way it fits the fanciest food. Pinot offers the perfect arena to measure your worldliness, and to make waves by creating a wine that is considered the domain of the French – any Francophile allusions are at a premium among the Stylists. For this reason, Bordeaux-style blends are also favoured, as is Chardonnay.

Complexity is good, and the simpler, brash varieties are not pursued. In the cellar, Stylists may be on top of all the latest technology, but will never allow this to dictate the higher truth that their grapes inevitably express, their originality. This is closely allied to the concept of terroir (see page 172), something Stylists (along with Individualists) are passionate about, and can discuss endlessly, which suits the Stylists' penchant for philosophising – these are the thinking persons' winemakers.

Now you know not to be surprised if the wines are strikingly expensive. A lot of thought has gone into them.

Hamilton Russell Vineyards

This winery exemplifies the Stylistic spirit to a tee. Their business is vineyards, and they happen to make wine. A collector of fine art, archaeological artefacts and cigars, Anthony Hamilton Russell continues where his pioneering father Tim left off. Their estate, in the auspiciously named Hemel en Aarde (Heaven and Earth) Valley has become, over the last few decades, a hallmark of fine style in many respects – and most notably in the exclusive nature of their range: Pinot Noir and Chardonnay.

Hemel en Aarde
Road (R320, off R43),
Hermanus
(028) 312 3595
Mon-Fri 9am-5pm, Sat
9am-1pm
Facilities ★ ★
Prices $$$

Turn off at the Hamilton Russell signpost and you will soon

see an imposing house on the hill, a statement of confidence that suits the prevailing attitude. The rather more down-to-earth tasting room houses the embodiment of this approach: olive oil from the land, honey from their bees, and their two wines. These are their vehicles in exploring origin-expressiveness.

The Hamilton Russell winery actually made the beautiful Hemel en Aarde Valley synonymous with Pinot Noir and Chardonnay by being among the first to plant these vines here in the early 1980s. It was a brave step, but taken on the back of firm research and an even firmer knowledge of the style of wine that they were after. These were firstly to be wines that reflected the essence of the place; or, in the words of owner Anthony Hamilton Russell, 'the expression of origin'. Secondly, they had to be Burgundian.

The Hemel en Aarde is a steep and winding valley, overlooked by impressive peaks. Its position means it's perfectly suited to funnel the winds from the very nearby sea which helps keep the valley cooler than many other Cape vineyards. And the clay-rich soils here are excellent for vines, expressing themselves as a refined minerality in the wines, in particular the demanding Burgundian varieties of Pinot Noir and Chardonnay.

The meticulous winemaking practice at HRV involves experiments like ageing the French oak staves for their barrels on the farm and then sending them back to France to be made into barrels (to imbibe the spirit of place). In the cellar, they have also been known to discard 10 tons from a 13-ton batch of Chardonnay grapes. And (of course) they carefully make the wine from each vineyard block separately, so that the particular style of each small piece of land is kept absolutely intact, and later blended according to the vision.

This is the way with Stylists. It's very refined and very deliberate. They gather respect because they are purists. To some people it may seem overly subtle, like playing with a pretentious idea. Yet the wine that is made here is universally considered exceptional. And does it capture the essence of heaven and earth? You decide.

pick of the wines

In their case it's easy because they only make two: a Pinot Noir and a Chardonnay.

Hamilton Russell Pinot Noir has become bolder and more opulent in recent years. It's justifiably seen as a benchmark South African Pinot Noir. Hamilton Russell Chardonnay is rich and characterised by mineral flavours that add complexity to the citrus fruit; this is more in the European style. You can also taste Southern Right Pinotage and Sauvignon Blanc at this cellar, both very good (and lower priced) wines.

while in the area

Do

♦ Whale-watching off the rocks at Hermanus, especially in August-September. The trail along the seaboard is beautiful even if the friendly mammals aren't about. Whale-watching hotline (028) 312 2629.

Eat

♦ Mogg's Country Cookhouse. Great country fare in a charming cottage high up the Hemel en Aarde Valley.

Follow the signs; it's past Hamilton Russell (028) 312 4321.

- ♦ Heaven. A great bistro overlooking the Hemel en Aarde at the neighbouring Newton Johnson winery (072) 905 3947.

Waterford Estate

The Stylists' penchant for a bit of philosophising is very evident in the person of Kevin Arnold, winemaker at Waterford Estate – and the Stylists' love for beautifully sensory environments is resoundingly clear in the evocative, fountain and lavender-infused Tuscan spaces of the winery.

Blaauwklippen Road, off R44, Stellenbosch
(021) 880-0496
Mon-Fri 9am-5pm, Sat 10am-1pm
Facilities ★ ★
Prices $ to $$$

Partner to Arnold is Jeremy Ord, not merely an IT mogul but clearly also a man of style and the means to bring said style to life. To build a winery to look just like an old Italian *piazza* is what you would expect from Stylists, surrounded as they are by endless Cape Dutch homesteads, and this harmonious winery has been designed to weather over the years and settle into the place that the owners visualised, looking like it's been there for centuries – in other words this is no ersatz effort, with results expected in weeks and months.

Waterford follows a code called 'The Waterford Way' which reinforces the idea that everything in life is interconnected and flowing, and not about a single season, harvest or vintage. This philosophy applies to their wine as to the environment. For many years, they planted vines and made wines, quietly assimilating information about their vineyards. Then, ten years after their first release, they presented The Jem, a multifaceted mélange of the red varieties on the farm. This is the art of blending taken to dizzying heights, an act of splendid creativity and style.

Stylistically, Arnold is focused on making wine that suits food. For him, wine can only be understood in its context, and this is at the table, with friends. His mantra is 'mouthfeel': the texture of the liquid in your mouth, its weight and balance as much as its flavour. This makes wine more like a type of food – very much akin to the European approach – and adds layers of complexity to the discussion of wine. And if the proof is in the eating, suffice to say that Waterford's wines are big hits with restaurant wine lists, something Arnold sees as highest praise.

'Making wine is not just about the here and now. It's about your whole life and the generations after,' is how Arnold describes his vision: an approach that looks back to his predecessors for lessons that others may easily discard just because they are 'old-fashioned'. At the same time, he happily works with modern techniques – a balancing act that takes the best from both worlds. The Waterford wines reflect this: like many modern wines, his are both soft and accessible and yet undeniably complex. The former a lesson of modernity; the latter the element that traditional wine styles are better known for.

▊ pick of the wines

Kevin Arnold Shiraz is a continuation of his previous successes with this variety at the Big Hitter Rust en Vrede. It's a balanced wine, made in the modern Shiraz style, with prominent fruit and smoky, spicy flavours. Sauvignon Blanc is a variety that has recently been turned into the most muscular of performers:

bold, bright and with powerful flavours to win awards and surprise consumers. Arnold has taken a different path, favouring texture above power. Waterford's is a rich, round, finessed wine, as is the Chardonnay.

while in the area

Do

* Try Waterford's tasting room coffee (after your wine tasting). They reckon it's the best in Stellenbosch.

Eat

* 96 Winery Road. Very good robust cooking with real flavours and a superb wine list. Off the R44 on Winery Road (021) 842-2020.

Morgenster Estate

The winery that is marked as a Stylist is often built on the vision of a single-minded individual – it can be more than one, but then they tend to have a single-minded and shared vision. Morgenster (Morning Star) Estate is a great example of

Lourensford Road,
Somerset West
(021) 852-1738
Mon-Fri 10am-5pm
Facilities ★ ★
Prices $$$

how powerful one man's vision can be. Part of erstwhile Cape governor W A van der Stel's stunning original farm some 300 years ago, and right alongside the famous Big Hitter Vergelegen (see page 44), it had, until the late-1990s, fallen off the wine map.

Along came a sprightly gent with an iron vision, an Italian soul and the wherewithal to turn dreams into reality. Giulio Bertrand is a Stylist in the original mould (it helps to be Italian), and he restored the fabulous and historic Cape Dutch home, filling it with art collectibles. He also transformed the estate into a serious red wine contender – along with a complementary line in award-winning olives and olive oils – by careful analysis of the soils and a desire to make world-class wines. The olive trees were a surprise addition, because the Helderberg landscape reminded Bertrand of his native Tuscany. Now Morgenster has one of the Cape's best olive tree nurseries and makes oils that win international awards.

When it comes to the wine, Bertrand's first reference (naturally) is first-growth Bordeaux, specifically St Emilion, which is French shorthand for the tricksy variety Cabernet Franc. So – as one does – he enlisted the aid of Pierre Lurton, the famous wine director of Chateau Cheval Blanc and Yquem, to groom his Cabernet Franc, Cabernet Sauvignon and Merlot into marvels of fine-tuned elegance. It's like hiring the design head of Ferrari.

After a few years, this winery's two Bordeaux-style blends were well entrenched in the awards circle. Just when it seemed this was the sum of it, Bertrand introduced a new range of Italian-inspired wines – the result of his experimental plantings of Nebbiolo and Sangiovese. Like the olive trees, what began as a trial soon proved that the Cape climate has a great deal in common with his native lands, and the Italian varieties thrived and soon proved too good to ignore.

This ridiculously picturesque estate with its steep terraces of vine and olive grove is today a wonderfully compact example of a historic Cape farm, with all the signature elements in place, and with the addition of a modern tasting room. Its position right alongside the Big Hitter Vergelegen offers a very interesting comparison of how two halves of one farm can be so different, and have such divergent characters.

pick of the wines

Morgenster Estate is a red blend of the classic three – Cabernet Sauvignon, Franc and Merlot – and a wine not to be taken lightly, though it slips down with supple ease. Lourens River Valley plays no second fiddle; it's just different in structure due to being mostly Merlot-based: a softer, riper variety. Both these wines would reward you if you stuck them in your cellar for a few years. Of the Italian reds, Nabucco is utterly decadent.

while in the area

Do

+ Visit the Helderberg Nature Reserve and explore the famous Cape fynbos along lovely mountain trails. www.helderbergnaturereserve.co.za

Eat

+ D'Vine Restaurant and Willowbrook Lodge is just around the corner and offers classically inspired cuisine in a garden setting (021) 851 3759 www.dvinerestaurant.co.za.

Other Noteworthy Stylists

La Motte

We've met the Rupert family before, visiting the impressive Anthonij Rupert Wines (pg 38) – and it is Hanneli Rupert-Koegelenberg, sister of Johann Rupert, who owns this glamorous and historic wine estate, also outside Franschhoek. Rupert-Koegelenberg's a world-renowned mezzo-soprano, and the estate holds regular classical music evenings and fine art exhibitions. They also grow rare flowers and have the world's largest private collection of disas – as well as cultivating organic oil-producing plants such as lavandine, rose geranium, Cape snow bush and buchu. Any doubt this is a Stylist of the finest pedigree?

R45 outside
Franschhoek
(021) 876-3119
Mon-Fri 9am-4.30pm,
Sat 10am-3pm
Facilities ★ ★ ★
Prices $$

La Motte, a famous name in Cape wine and home to beautiful heritage buildings, had fallen on leaner times until it was purchased by the Rupert family and carefully restored from the 1970s onwards. For a time, its sales and marketing were handled by a large corporate, but, in the spirit of a Stylist, they rebelled against the idea that their wine should be bottled off site. Marketing's one thing, but when making a wine it should be cared for at home – all the way into the bottle. So it was merely a matter of time before all the winery's operations were again under the personal care of the family, and the last decade has seen a sharpening of focus on quality and on specific varieties like Shiraz and Sauvignon Blanc.

2009 saw the estate mark 25 years of Shiraz production, and the early 2000s saw the launch of the Pierneef Collection (Pierneef was a famous South African grand master painter) which included a Shiraz-Viognier and an exciting Shiraz-Grenache blend in fine, and very stylish, livery.

🍷 pick of the wines

Their Pierneef Sauvignon Blanc is organically grown on their Bot River vineyards and this is a fine example of the variety. It's focused and fresh, but with gently luscious edges. La Motte Shiraz is very good, very silky in texture; and their Chardonnay is one of the most perfectly drinkable and balanced examples of this grape you are likely to find.

Waterkloof

In look a Futurist, this new winery, perched on the brow of a dramatic hill, is an architectural marvel, filled with the highest quality winemaking equipment, glass and steel and wood. However, in contrast to the *du jour* talk of optimal ripeness, maximum extraction and new French oak,

Sir Lowry's Pass Road, off N2, Somerset West
(021) 873-2418
Mon-Fri 9am-4.30pm,
Sat and Sun 10am-3pm
Facilities ★ ★ ★
Price $$

owner Paul Boutinot and winemaker Werner Engelbrecht first talk about making wines that they'd like to drink themselves. For Boutinot, this means a wine of balance, a wine that is more reflective of the place it comes from than the grape it's made from, or indeed the yeasts used to ferment these grapes. Stylists to the core.

On the farm, they are returning to bio-dynamic and traditional vineyard management. As Boutinot is quick to point out, it was only from the 1960s on that farming became fertiliser-led and production driven. Until then the phases of the moon set the pace, not yields. So there's more to learn in tradition. In the cellar, too, they use natural and not cultivated yeasts to give them longer and hotter fermentations – this to 'blow off' the estery aromas and flavours that can play a very dominant role in a young wine's profile but then soon depart to leave the wine so much poorer.

A key example serves to illustrate their firmly Stylistic approach. As the pinnacle of their Sauvignon Blanc range, the Waterkloof Sauvignon Blanc was not released in 2007. Not because 2007 was a poor vintage, but because it was too expressive and excessively fruity and therefore did not create a wine of balance. When most wineries are pumping flavours to garner medals, this is a fascinating step into another paradigm.

pick of the wines

Sauvignon Blanc is a favoured variety here (they have one in each of their three wine tiers), and the Circumstance Sauvignon Blanc is a fantastic example of how much mouthfeel this variety can achieve. Their Viognier is also one of the Cape's best examples (South African Viognier is often far too alcoholic); while their Merlot and Shiraz are both fine reds, with lovely food tannins.

Bouchard Finlayson

With names like Kaaimansgat (Crocodile's Lair), Galpin Peak (the mountain peak that rises above the farm) and Hannibal (the Carthaginian general), Bouchard Finlayson's wines paint a very colourful picture. These names are rich with suggestion and allusions, in particular to the places that the grapes come from, so it comes as little surprise that Peter Finlayson is one of the original Stylists of the Hemel en Aarde Valley, and the pioneer of Pinot Noir.

Hemel en Aarde
Road (R320, off R43),
Hermanus
(028) 312-3515
Mon-Fri 9am-5pm, Sat
9.30am-12.30pm
Facilities ★ ★ ★
Prices $$$

More than any other winemaker in the Cape, Finlayson gathers the epithet of 'philosophical'. Perhaps it's his steely eyes, trademark beard and big stature, but the reason is more likely to be his economy with words and habit of answering questions with analogies to sports, music or poetry. Anything but wine, which can be quite frustrating if you are a wine journalist.

So he likens winemaking not to an artistic creation, where you begin, think, dream, work again, eat, work, etc; but to a big sports match where you run on to the field with everyone watching you and play your heart out for the duration of the game (the harvest period) until the final whistle blows. You only have one chance, and you have to make it happen right there, right then.

Well, his goal average is pretty high. After more than 21 vintages of working with Pinot Noir and Chardonnay, Bouchard Finlayson's examples of these wines are consistently world class.

But this Stylist is also something of a maverick, as is exemplified in his creation of the curiously named Hannibal: a wine where Italian varieties are vinified in Africa – the opposite of an African in Italy.

♦ pick of the wines

Tête de Cuvée Galpin Peak Pinot Noir is a mouthful any way you approach it. The best wine from the best years are put into the best barrels ... this is the business and their Pinot Noir has been deemed best in the world. Missionvale Chardonnay is unlike the flashy Chardonnays that fill shelves: a true sophisticate in firm Stylist tradition.

...Fact...

The average age of a French oak tree harvested for use in wine barrels is 170 years.

DEMOCRATS

'A business that makes nothing but money is a poor kind of business.'

– Henry Ford

Wine is dogged by the perception that it's a fancy beverage, at fancy prices. Unfortunately, this perception, as it relates to prices, is often true. Wine, for a variety of reasons (see page 174), is an expensive drink – but this is relative. If you consider that wine is most often not mass-produced and that it tells more of a story of the place it comes from (unlike your average soda), prices start making more sense. Wine is the product of local farmers and the fields you see around you. The tending of vines is painstaking, and often a gamble with nature. Therefore it will cost more.

Having said this, every wine region in the world has its bargains: wines that are loved for their happy disposition, combining satisfying drinking with friendly prices. These are the everyday, easy wines that are on more tables and taken to more parties than their serious siblings – the wines that people like to live with from day to day. Call them table wines, call them vin ordinaire, even call them plonk – almost everyone drinks them.

Wineries that have always remained true to the people, and that have consistently made good wine at great prices are the Democrats. Here, quality outstrips the price time and again. The tasting rooms often feel homely, they're certainly not Corporate. They are often found a bit further away from the glamorous wine hubs like Stellenbosch and Franschhoek, and they are often cooperatives – collectives of farmers working together. Areas like Paarl, Worcester, Rawsonville and Robertson have historically been the heartlands of these collectives.

Punters want the happy medium between quality and price because we aren't always looking for a religious experience in the wine glass, but nor do we ever want a hideous one. The Democrats have a track record of making good drinking wines at fair prices. They can be trusted, they are reliable and consistent. And, with the constant improvement of all the wines of the Cape, they also make a greater and greater number of really good wines. So don't be surprised to get more than you bargained for. The Democrats are not here because they are the cheapest; rather because they're great quality wines at prices you wouldn't expect.

Villiera Wines

If ever there was a winery defined by its owners, it's the laid-back and friendly Villiera, where the Grier family farms. If ever there was an award for making quality wines at decent prices, it would be covered with the same name. Villiera Wines has consistently been making award-winning wines and has never let this

R304 at Koelenhof interchange (exit 39 off N1)
(021) 865-2002
Mon-Fri 8.30am-5pm, Sat 8.30am-1pm
Facilities ★ ★
Prices $ to $$

become an excuse for gratuitous price hiking. It's about honest winemaking here, and prices that are modesty incarnate. One of those places you find and can't believe it's true – and then you go back (and back) and it's still the same! For their generosity of winemaking spirit with no lack of sheer quality, this is a jewel in the Democratic crown.

Jeff Grier is the self-effacing production chief who's been making wine here for over twenty years, and was a pioneer in sparkling wine in South Africa. These bubblies quickly became multi-medal winners; and still the family felt no need to inject any Botox into the prices while other wineries swelled price tags on the merest whiff of judges' gold.

Villiera is a winery with a supremely democratic range, from some more unusual wines like Gewürztraminer to the standard bearers like Cabernet Sauvignon, through sweet wines and a range of limited releases that go under the category 'Cellar Door' (a reward to those who make the visit). Then there are the Cap Classiques that they're famous for, sparkling wines that consistently rate among the Cape's best, and sell at the price of a moderate red – incredible if you consider the effort that goes into the making of a Champagne-style sparkling wine that goes through a second fermentation inside the bottle, one of the most labour-intensive operations known to a cellar rat. These bubblies age beautifully too.

Their bubbly innovations also led to the Brut Natural, a wine made with natural yeasts and no sulphur additions. It's a wine that illustrates their awareness of new trends in consumer preference as well as the attention they spend on eco-friendly vineyard management – you can't make wine without preservatives like sulphur unless your fruit is very clean and healthy.

If you have little time and want to stock up on a range of

wines, knowing that you are getting the absolute best for your buck, this is the place for you. The small, homely tasting room on the property lacks any pretence. You can also go along with a picnic, buy a few bottles of the ambrosial bubbly, and take some time off on the lawns. No worries. And if Anton Smal, the winemaker, isn't around, you can be sure he's off looking for some surf.

pick of the wines

Villiera Tradition Brut is the ideal anytime bubbly. The Monro Brut is made to be more full-bodied; a creamier style. Sauvignon Blanc is a signature wine here in the green fruit mode, while the Chenin Blanc shows lovely balanced yellow fruit with just enough body from some wood maturation. Down to Earth Red is a bargain quaffer and perfect for Italian meals. At the other end of the spectrum, their flagship Monro is sleek and plump for laying down awhile. But grab whatever you fancy; the wines are very consistent.

while in the area

Eat

- At Joostenberg Deli, where the food is streets ahead of most plush-looking places: real country cooking by a top French chef at very relaxed prices. Also one of the best places for cold meats, breads and real farm produce. Turn off the N1 at the R304, then a right turn (021) 884-4208.

Méthode Cap Classique

'Champagne' can legally only refer to the sparkling wine that is made in France in the traditional manner – by a second fermentation inside the bottle itself. Méthode Cap Classique is the name we in South Africa use to describe wines made in precisely this manner. Wine is the product of a single fermentation; MCC is made by going through two (after more sugar and yeast are added), and the released carbon dioxide from this second ferment is trapped in the bottle. This is what gives it the dense and delicate bubble. It is not carbonated or made in bulk tanks – each and every bottle is its own fermentation vessel. The only (still big) difference between MCC and Champagne is that it is made here, not there, invoking the vital role that 'terroir' (see page 172) plays.

Delheim

Up a pretty panhandle valley road and past the deeply atmospheric Muratie (see page 152), you get to the perennially popular Delheim, another winery with oodles of character. In fact, this valley road offers fantastic old world charm, and if you're pushed for time on your Stellenbosch visit, come here.

Knorhoek Road, off R44
(021) 888-4600
Mon-Fri 9am-5pm, Sat 9am-3.30pm, Sun (Oct-Apr) 10.30am-3.30pm
Facilities ★ ★ ★
Prices $ to $$

Delheim is an estate that has been visitor-friendly since 1971 when they were the first Cape winery to open a tasting centre and this helped blaze the way for modern Cape wine tourism. Today, the estate has a popular and pretty country garden restaurant where farmyard fowl loiter and the family's dogs ask politely for snacks. There's also a curio and pottery shop, all with a homely brick and ivy look, and you can prepare to fight through happy crowds in season.

Not short of innovation, another idea the family came up with was to sell tasting glasses – legendary winemaker Spatz Sperling's wife Vera said she decided on this because she 'couldn't stand the thought of washing another glass'. Materfamilias Vera pops up again in the name of one of their flagship wines, Vera Cruz – a reference, allegedly, to the cross that Vera has had to bear: her husband's wine obsession. Vera Cruz is in fact the estate's finest vineyard, the source of intensely fruited grapes.

Further evidence of the friendly approach is at the entrance to the vineyard, where rows of different vines from around the world are introduced for your perusal, along with old farm implements, retired here with signs that tell you what they were used for. In the tasting room you'll find jars of winemaking additives also with explanations – strangely science class-ish, but great as a way to learn about how wine is, and was, made.

Son Victor ranges the farm as viticulturist, and quite a job it is, with fifteen varieties planted on 148 hectares. Their range of wines is Catholic as a result, and incorporates simple table wines to the estate heavyweights and on to stickies, including the famous 'Spatzendreck' – not named after the father but, rather colourfully, the sparrows' droppings after the birds have feasted on these sweet late harvest grapes. Delheim's wines are collectively excellent, and at great prices. The very atmospheric brickskeller tasting room also has a separate section where you can find aged wines and collectibles – they made their first wine in 1961.

Delheim are deeply committed conservationists, and have energetically preserved swathes of natural fynbos on their farm, donated land towards the creation of a nature reserve, created a water-recycling wetland, and introduced lighter bottles to lower their carbon footprint. So even more reason to feel good about drinking their wine!

♦ pick of the wines

The Sauvignon Blanc-Chenin Blanc and the Dry Red are as good as any unassuming table wines at the price – with all the bits in the right place. The Chardonnay Sur Lie is made in a rich buttery style for lovers of wood flavours. The Shiraz is generous and smoky and the Grand Reserve is definitely more austere: the extrovert and the introvert. Quite a step up in price is the Vera Cruz Shiraz, but well worth flexing the credit card for.

while in the area

Do

+ Hikes in the adjacent Klapmutskop Conservancy, including alluring full-moon hikes. Details at www.dirtopia. co.za

Eat

+ At the on-site Delheim Restaurant, where traditional Cape cuisine meets German favourites in a very relaxed, countrified atmosphere (021) 888 4607.

Hartenberg Estate

A Democrat of long-standing is Stellenbosch's Hartenberg Estate.

Some may remember the days of their 'Bin' wines which consistently over-delivered in quality, and the spirit of these lives on in the restaurant evergreens – Hartenberg Cabernet Sauvignon-Shiraz and Sauvignon Blanc. Over the years,

Off M23 (Bottelary Rd)
(021) 865-2541
Mon-Fri 9am-5pm, Sat 10am-3pm; Sundays (Dec-Easter) 10am-3.30pm
Facilities ★ ★ ★
Prices $ to $$$

they have worked hard to elevate the quality of their range and now it has to be said that the prices of their top wines have not so much crept as strolled right on up, but value for money has remained certain.

Now also gone is the famous Pontac (a historic Cape variety that Hartenberg were the last to bottle) but the cellar still persists, happily, with another of winemaker Carl Schultz's favourites, Riesling – a variety that is in danger of becoming extinct in the Cape. Theirs is consistently good, slightly sweet but never cloying. Hartenberg have, however, become justly famous for their Shiraz and Merlot, the former in a rich and voluptuous style, the latter ultra-silky and accomplished. Top of the pops is the Gravel Hill Shiraz, from a crazy vineyard where the vines seem to rise solely out of loose, jagged rocks, with no soil in sight. As far as visual evidence of 'terroir' goes, this is hard to beat.

And then there are the newer 'family' wines, named after their founding forebears, which are very serious wines indeed (as the definite article in their names suggests): The Stork, The Mackenzie and The Eleanor.

In summary, there is something for everyone on the wine side, from casual to very serious. But this venerable history of making good wines is matched by a tasting room experience that's among the friendliest in the Cape, and wines are all presented without any pretence. Add to this the fantastic and legendary vintner's lunches – picnics in the garden in summer and robust soups in winter – and you have an estate that draws and keeps customers.

Care for the environment has also resulted in a lovely trail that winds around the beautiful wetland on the farm (occupying 65 hectares of the farm's 170), and twitchers are lavishly entertained by the variety of birds, including rare species like Burchell's Coucal as well as three breeding pairs of Spotted Eagle Owl. Fish Eagles visit in summer.

Hartenberg hosts regular events on the farm, with music and all-round family pursuits (look out for these on their website), and when you visit be sure to go and take a look the entrance to their underground cellar – the heavy door here with its oversized keyhole was originally the Castle of Cape Town's main point of entry – making this the oldest door in South Africa.

🍾 pick of the wines

At the budget end, the Cabernet Sauvignon-Shiraz is smooth and easy for anytime drinking. Taking quite a few steps up, your cellar definitely requires some Hartenberg Shiraz, the regular and the fantastic Gravel Hill, if you can secure some of this limited release wine. The Eleanor Chardonnay is a sublime white that's richly wooded and needs a good few years to show at its best.

while in the area

Do

♦ The walk along their scenic wetland (discuss with tasting room) – you can also take a picnic lunch along to enjoy en route.

Eat

♦ Right here, just be sure to call ahead to book one of the delicious baskets.

Other
Noteworthy
Democrats

Joostenberg Wines

Democrats typically have a lot going on for the visitor, they're tourist-friendly stops that go well beyond just a line-up of wines to taste while making the appropriate noises of appreciation. Joostenberg, however, takes the cake. There is a plant nursery, a pottery shop, Balinese furniture, a deli with lovely breads and goodies, a butchery that makes some of the best pork charcuterie in the Cape, and an excellent bistro where French chef Christophe cooks amazing food at perfect prices. And to top it all, the farm is only a short drive outside the city, just off the highway.

Klein Joostenberg, R304 off N1 highway
(021) 884-4932
Daily 10am-5pm
Facilities ★★★
Prices $ to $$

And all these charms before we even get to the delightful wines that Tyrrel Myburgh makes here on this, his family farm. He's something of a Shiraz and Chenin Blanc nut, with a penchant for Viognier as a blending component (he reminds of similarities between the climate here and that of the Rhône). He's also serious about going back to the roots through sustainable farming that is moving ever more towards organic principles for wines that are 'more genuine'.

'Genuine' is a great word for this operation, the essence of a real working farm (now over 250 years old) where the whole family is involved in one form or another and absolute modesty is the response to the praise they get for the fine wine and food that emanates from the land.

pick of the wines

The Fairhead is a white blend that features Chenin Blanc, Viognier and Grenache Blanc and is a textured and delightful drink, great with food. The Shiraz-Viognier is beautifully balanced and refreshingly not in the blockbuster style at all, while their Chenin Blanc Noble Late Harvest is simply breathtakingly rich and complex.

Welbedacht

Otherwise, and popularly, known as Schalk Burger & Sons, this farm in Wellington makes a great range of expressive and well-priced wines but is even more famous as the home of two of South Africa's rugby legends – Schalk Burger Senior and Junior ('Groot' and 'Klein' Schalk; though Junior is also a behemoth of a man and a Springbok flanker feared by opposition teams the world over).

Take Oakdene Road off R44 between Wellington and Ceres
(021) 873-1877
Mon-Fri 8.30am-5pm, Sat 9am-2pm
Facilities ★ ★
Prices $ to $$$

Schalk Senior had a successful career in the world of corporate wineries, and then started the family winery in 2003 with immense gusto, ably and equally enthusiastically assisted by son Tiaan. Visitors to the farm are warmly welcomed by the family, which includes a number of Shar-pei dogs. Wellington is a little way off the usual wine tour map, but this means two things: generally friendlier prices and the spirit of old-school hospitality that South African farmers have a deserved reputation for. I can't speak for the dogs, though they were tolerant enough when I was there.

Starting with the 'Meerkat' range of wines, this winery over-delivers in quality. These are designed as easy drinkers, with lovely expressive fruit and soft tannins. The Welbedacht range continues the house style of juicy and well-rounded wines; while the Proprietor's Reserve range pulls no punches in terms of opulence. All the wines maintain a lovely fruit purity, they've not been masked by overt wood styling. There's actually an elegance to them – something that would not be suggested by judging the physically imposing Burger family on looks alone.

ᛁ pick of the wines

Meerkat Pinotage for fruit delight, the Welbedacht Cabernet Sauvignon Barrique Select for more elegance in the traditional style. The Cricket Pitch hints at the family's sports madness and this wine is a lovely, balanced blend of predominantly Merlot and Cabernet Sauvignon with fine tannins. If the budget allows, the flagship No. 6 is a statement wine with equally impressive packaging.

Van Loveren Private Cellar

The Robertson region is bountifully Democrat territory. The warmth of the valley and its historic affinity to winemaking coupled with enthusiastic production means that there is a good deal of quality wine at stress-free prices. Van Loveren is a farm that has typified this approach

R317 between
Robertson and
Bonnievale
(023) 615-1505
Mon-Fri 8.30am-5pm,
Sat 9.30am-1pm
Facilities ★★
Prices $ to $$

for decades. The relaxed and beautiful tasting area is in a traditional 'rondavel', a round hut amid the bright red flowers of the garden. It's a pleasure to visit, and pleasure is what this farm is all about.

Like so many Democrats, the farm began by making sweet wines and then expanded – widely – to begin to make the eclectic variety that's a hallmark of the cellar. This is a family-run operation, and the Retiefs are moving along the generations but keeping the tradition of making wines for anyone, anytime – no better exemplified than by the 1.5-litre Four Cousins wines. The picture of the gregarious family on the label leaves you in no doubt what these are all about: wine that's for friends and good times.

The early introduction of cold fermentation facilities began their expansion into good white wines, and today they make all the whites you've heard of and then some, like nearly forgotten Colombard. They don't neglect the red either … and now also make a range of Limited Release wines with more gravitas. But the heart of this winery remains easy-going wines that aren't structured to be kept for a decade: they're made to drink right here, right now, whenever the mood strikes.

◖ pick of the wines

Your choice from a reliably soft and fruity range for instant pleasure. The Cabernet Sauvignon-Shiraz is packed with good varietal flavours and is honestly dry; the Wolverine Creek Shiraz Reserve is soft and full of dark, juicy fruit. The ultimate anytime red remains the supple and sweetish River Red. On the white side, the Sauvignon Blanc is your best bet, while the Pinot Grigio is a fantastic quaffer, pleasantly dry and refreshing.

Do you drink with your eyes?

While most of us would like to think that 'we drink what we like' when it comes to wine, science is against us. It appears that the price tag plays a decisive role in how much we like a wine. A study conducted by researchers at the USA's National Institutes of Health used MRI brain imagery to conclude that 'increasing the price of a wine increases subjective reports of flavour pleasantness as well as blood-oxygen-level-dependent activity in [the] medial orbitofrontal cortex, an area that is widely thought to encode for experienced pleasantness during experiential tasks.' In other words, we mostly drink with our eyes firmly on the price tag. Sad, but true. Marketers everywhere must be thrilled that price and perceived status actually makes the wine taste better for us drinkers.

Put it this way: it would take a very confident (or wealthy) man to slate the 2006 Domaine Liger-Belair La Romanée he's just paid R8250 a bottle for! (At 2009 prices…).

OLD SPICE

The joys and rewards of cellaring fine red wines

One of the unique selling points of good red wine is the promise that it will age gracefully. You'll often read about this on the back label, or the marketer will guarantee delight to those who hoard and resist the temptation of premature uncorking. 'Will continue to improve for 10 years or more', or some such assurance, adds immeasurably to the allure of a wine. This is essentially why we ascribe greater value to red wine than white wine.

The reality, even with an iron-willed ability to resist early drinking, is somewhat different. Many of our red wines do not age (in the sense of continuing to improve) for much over five or six years. This is because much has changed in winemaking over the last twenty-odd years. Cape wine is no longer made in the way it was before 1994. It is less tannic, it's softer and more approachable in its youth, and the corollary is that it does not mature and improve for as long. In the old style of winemaking (still practised in many parts of Europe), a red wine is hard and unapproachable in its youth, with a tannic and leathery texture.

After five years it's beginning to be drinkable, but it's only soft and smooth after ten. 'Modern' winemaking, where the fruit is picked riper and handled very softly, and where tannins are velvety from careful extraction, results in wine that can invariably be drunk as soon as it's released. Sure, these wines do age, but they are 'pre-integrated' and age is often not a prerequisite to further pleasure. Plus they will not go the same distance. In many ways, the red that really needs a decade to reach optimal drinking is now a relic of another era ...

What you need to look for if you are interested in putting wines away is a cellar with a track record of making age-worthy wines. These cellars either work with grapes that are more suited to maturation (Cabernet Sauvignon and its blends) or their philosophy of winemaking leads them to create wines with legs. Secondly, you need to pick a vintage that will go the distance. Not all vintages are equal in this ability, and the Cape is a diverse terrain. For example, growing conditions in 2007 were excellent for Durbanville but less favourable for Stellenbosch. So watch out for generalisations about the vintage and rather get your information from a good wine retailer.

Which Cape vintages are good for keeping?

- 1968, 1969
- 1974, 1976, 1978, 1979
- 1984, 1986, 1989
- 1995, 1997, 1998
- 2001, 2003, 2007

Which producers make wines to cellar?

Some options:

Annandale, Boekenhoutskloof Winery, Buitenverwachting, Grangehurst, Kanonkop Estate, Le Riche, Meerlust Estate, Morgenhof, Neil Ellis, Sadie Family, Simonsig Wine Estate, Thelema Mountain Vineyards, Vergenoegd

Where can I buy older wine?

Specialist wine retailers like Norman Goodfellows (011 788-4814) and Caroline's Fine Wines (021 419-8984) are good places to ask after wine collections for sale or older vintages. You can also contact Bergkelder's Vinoteque Wine Bank (021 809-8283) for vintage Stellenbosch wine.

Classic and collectible wines in South African history

- *GS Cabernet 1968* – A legendary wine which a Wine Spectator senior editor recently gave an unprecedented (for South Africa) 95-point rating. Made from Durbanville fruit and almost impossible to get hold of.
- *Lanzerac Pinotage 1969* – In the original 'skittle' bottle, these early Pinotages were made from Stellenbosch fruit, and in big vats, never small French oak. They age magnificently.
- *Fairview Pinotage 1974* – An early independent-producer wine for the Cape, made by Cyril Back and still tasting very good indeed.
- *Nederburg Private Bin Cabernet Sauvignon 1974* – A very famous wine from a very famous Cape vintage. As good as anything made in Bordeaux.
- *Hamilton Russell Pinot Noir 1986* – In 1990, the

John Platter guide said this wine 'has obvious charm' and after tasting it very recently, I would say the charm is still there, though now subtle.

- *Kanonkop Paul Sauer 1986* – Across in Stellenbosch, another classic from this vintage, massively concentrated and with firm tannins in its youth, slowly relaxing as it ages over the decades.
- *Boekenhoutskloof Syrah 1997* – From a vineyard that has now been completely grubbed up, this Syrah has set a benchmark for the variety locally. Over ten years on, it's still got lots to teach us.

'I do not want to deconstruct the pleasure of wine by trying to work out whether the aromas smell of bananas or apricots. If you analyse too much, you end up destroying the pleasure.'

– Lionel Poilane, famous French baker

WAYS THROUGH THE WINELANDS

These are not your conventional wine routes that lead you through geographical regions; these routes lead you by what you're interested in. Travelling the winelands is after all never only about wine – it's also about the places, the food and the action. So double your fun and entertainment. All of the places listed offer the combination of both good wine (the wine farm is in bold/italics) and more at the same location.

The Good Food Trails

Most would agree that eating is part of the winelands experience, so eating well has to be even better. There is a growing trend to winery-restaurants, and many of the Cape's best chefs have moved into the winelands or have opened a second restaurant here. Here is a pick of the really interesting restaurants.

The Franschhoek Trail

AKA the 'wine is good but food is better' trail, because of the general quality of the restaurants in this valley. You will have to stay a few days or make return visits to make the most of this trail; it's not so easy to pack more than one of these visits into a single day.

- Lunch at *La Petite Ferme*. Not only has this quaint spot got incredible views and good country fare on the menu, it also boasts a tiny winery right next door to the restaurant that supplies much of the restaurant's wines. Mark Dendy Young is the winemaker (it's a Dendy Young family affair here) and the wines are accomplished, in particular the Chardonnay and the Merlot. The lawns are tailored for after-lunch lazing.

  > Pass Road
  > (021) 876-3016
  > Mon-Sun lunch only
  > $$

- Gourmandising with bubbles at *Haute Cabrière*. Set into the mountainside, this cave-like restaurant is also a wine maturation cellar and the place has a cathedral-like feeling. Achim von Arnim, a local legend, makes the wines. Of particular mention is his range of bubblies that he loves to open the traditional way – with a cavalry sword. All the dishes are offered in main or starter portions for sampling, and all are matched to the cellar's wines.

Pass Road
(021) 876-3688
Mon-Sun lunch and dinner
$$$

• Home-made flavour at *Bread & Wine*. On the Môreson wine farm, this restaurant's name says it all. They bake the best breads, combine this with home-cured meats and fresh ingredients, and serve it with the cheerful wine of the farm. This is about good and tasty country food.

Happy Valley Road
(021) 876-3692
Wed-Sun lunch and dinner
$$

• French at *Mon Plaisir at Chamonix*. As French bistros go, this one is as real as they get. Run by Celine and David in a personal fashion, you can expect lots of duck on the menu, while the wines here are really good, especially the Chardonnay and Pinot Noir.

Uitkyk Street
(021) 876-2393
Wed-Sat lunch and dinner, Sun lunch
$$

• Picnics at *Boschendal*. Picnics and more at this old Cape favourite, with its rolling lawns and gazebos. The more formal option with Cape dishes is lunch buffet-style inside the historic old wine cellar. The wines made here are extensive and of good quality. The place can become very busy over season with tour groups.

> R310 between Stellenbosch and Franschhoek
> (021) 870-4274
> Seven days a week
> $$

The Constantia Trail

This is the cradle of the Cape wine scene and, fittingly, there are also a number of wonderful restaurants on wine farms in this superbly graceful part of the peninsula. Also favourable is its proximity to Cape Town itself.

- Formal dining at *Buitenverwachting*. The farm makes consistently superior wines, which the restaurant matches with precise cuisine and very good service in a reserved, somewhat conservative environment. During the day, there's a more informal terrace menu. Picnics on summer days on the lovely lawn are highly recommended too.

> Klein Constantia Road
> (021) 794-3522
> Tues-Fri lunch and dinner, Sat dinner only
> $$$

- Contemporary cuisine at *La Colombe*. One of the country's best chefs plays at this pretty garden restaurant. The venue is informal, but the world-class food is exquisitely plated and irresistibly flavoured; the service is sure. Plus the outside seating is idyllic on a summer's day and the wines are good, notably the Sémillon and 'White' and 'Red'.

> Constantia Uitsig, Spaanschemat River Road
> (021) 794-2390
> Mon-Sun lunch and dinner, except Sun eve in winter
> $$$

• *Bistro Sixteen82* at Steenberg Vineyards in Constantia is a beautiful space in a chic, contemporary style, flowing off the tasting room. The menu is happily diverse and geared for brunch and lunch only: from charcuterie platters to good pastas, most dishes are available in small or large portions.

> Steenberg Road
> (021) 713 2211
> Open daily 9am-8pm

• Cape traditional at *Groot Constantia Estate*. This home of Cape winemaking features two restaurants. *Jonkershuis* is in a lovely historic space and serves Cape country fare, while *Simon's* is a more contemporary café. Both are reliable.

> Groot Constantia Road
> Jonkershuis (021) 794-6255
> Mon-Sat breakfast, lunch and dinner, Sun lunch
> $$
>
> Simon's (021) 794 1143
> Mon-Sun lunch, dinner Tues-Sat, breakfast in season
> $

The Stellenbosch Trail

This is the heart of the Cape wine world, and many of the wineries have lovely café-style venues or bistros that are great for a casual meal, but if you want more serious food, try here:

- Real country cooking at *96 Winery Road*. Owned by out-and-out wine and food men and next to Ken Forrester Wines, this is the unofficial capital of the winelands food experience. It's hearty comfort food here, with an eye on seasonality and a fun-loving wine list, featuring the very good Forrester wines.

  Winery Road, off R44 near Somerset West
  (021) 842-2020
  Mon-Sat lunch and dinner, Sun lunch only
  $$

- Refined contemporary at *Terroir*. Michael Broughton's cooking is both powerful and profound at this upscale bistro. The menu changes to reflect what is in season and the service is relaxed, as is the Mediterranean space that it's in. Great wines, led by Chenin Blanc and Cabernet Sauvignon.

  Kleine Zalze Winery, off R44
  (021) 880-8167
  Mon-Sat lunch and dinner, Sun lunch
  $$$

- Cutting edge at *Overture*. Bertus Basson is a young chef with masses of energy and the desire to create the best in contemporary cuisine, with a serious respect for local and organic produce. The venue features staggering views, and the service is good.

> Hidden Valley Winery, Annandale Road
> (021) 808-5959
> Tues-Sat lunch and dinner
> $$

- Refined elegance at *Rust en Vrede*. The most serene restaurant in the Cape, and one of the leading restaurants in the country, this is the home of chef David Higgs' wonderful cuisine. A fine dining occasion, you can expect the best of everything here at this world-class experience.

> Rust en Vrede Estate, Annandale Road
> (021) 881-3881
> Tues-Sat dinner
> $$$

- High drama at *Tokara*. You will not find a more spectacular setting for a winery or restaurant in these parts. The food has also been known to cause a few stirs for its provocative ingredient pairings. Very modern, very chic.

> Helshoogte Pass Road between Stellenbosch and Franschhoek
> (021) 808-5959
> Tues-Sat lunch and dinner
> $$$

- Contemporary wonder at *Delaire Graff*. Only the most collectable art and striking decor for this revamped winery with its modern restaurant. The deck offers staggering views, while the interior is a delight. The menu features serious twists on well-known comfort dishes.

> Delaire Graff Estate
> Helshoogte Pass Road between Stellenbosch and Franschhoek
> (021) 885-8181
> Tues-Sun lunch, Tues-Sat dinner
> $$$

- Modern French at *Waterkloof*. Spectacular views and an engineering marvel of a winery host this understated restaurant where the food follows suit – unfussy but excellent.

> Waterkloof Winery, Sir Lowry's Pass Road
> (021) 858 1292
> Mon-Sat lunch and dinner, Sun lunch
> $$

- Country delights at *Joostenberg Deli*. Real country cooking in a down-to-earth setting with some of the best charcuterie, breads and real farm produce.

> Klein Joostenberg. Turn off the N1 at the R304, then a right turn
> (021) 884-4208
> Tues-Sun breakfast, lunch
> $

- Modern eclectic at *Cuvée*. This striking and

contemporary restaurant offers some very unusual food and also good modern revisions of classic Cape fare.

> Simonsig Wine Estate, Kromme Rhee Road,
> Koelenhof, between R44 & R304
> (021) 888-4932

• Elevated seasonal cuisine at *Jordan Restaurant* with George Jardine. Jardine is the award-winning chef of the eponymous restaurant in Cape Town, and now the winelands also has a chance to showcase his exciting cuisine at this fine winery (see page 76).

> Jordan Wine Estate, Stellenbosch Kloof Road,
> Vlottenberg
> (021) 881-3612 restaurant@jordanwines.com
> Tues-Fri lunch, Thurs & Fri dinner

The Scenic Trails

If you want a beautiful drive with a few top wineries to pop in on along the way, here are a few of the best ones. Of course, the whole of the Cape winelands is fantastically picturesque with idyllic pastoral scenes around every corner, so the most important consideration is: don't be in a rush.

The Helshoogte Pass Road (R310)

This is a dramatic pass road that links Stellenbosch with

Franschhoek. The climb up from Stellenbosch is steep as you move right up to Tokara, Thelema Mountain Vineyards and Delaire, all of which are worthwhile wine stops. After these, the road flattens somewhat into the Banhoek Valley where you will find the modern Zorgvliet winery. Then you descend to the pretty mountain village of Pniel, where you can stop and ask a local what the name means. On to the linking road to Franschhoek; on your right you'll come across the sweeping hectares of Boschendal Wines before joining the R45 and travelling right past some of the grand old Franschhoek estates like Anthonij Rupert Wines and La Motte, as well as the Futurist Graham Beck Wines.

Through Franschhoek itself, you can continue left up another pass road (Franschhoek Pass, home to restaurants Haute Cabrière and La Petite Ferme) with its incredible views looking back over the town and places to stop and have a look – and if you keep going on this spectacular road you'll reach a huge dam, the Theewaterskloof. Take a right here and make your way back to Cape Town via Grabouw and Somerset West.

The Sir Lowry's Pass Road to Hermanus (N2)

After you have survived the arduous, stop-start section through Somerset West up the mountain you will have spectacular views of False Bay and then you'll plunge into the deciduous fruit vales at the back of Elgin where a number of farm stalls and coffee shops tempt. You'll pass Oak Valley Wines (a good stop) and then the Paul Cluver Estate. Down the Houwhoek Pass, you take the Hermanus off-ramp (R43) and before long make a worthwhile back track by turning left to Bot River to visit Beaumont Wines (see page 93), Luddite and Wildekrans. Back on the road to Hermanus, and left before you begin to head into the sprawling town itself, up into the Hemel en Aarde Valley, a deep and steep one that rises and rises, offering amazing riches for the wine-lover: the stylish Hamilton Russell Vineyards and Bouchard Finlayson first, further up you'll find the up-and-coming Newton-Johnson cellar (with its great Heaven restaurant) and Sumaridge, then Ataraxia and Creation Wines. Back down you come, take the road in to the town of Hermanus where you can look for whales if it's spring – the town is justly famous as a spotting site with its cliff-side walks and vantages. An alternative road back from Hermanus that doesn't take in Sir Lowry's Pass is the awesome coastal road past Kleinmond and Pringle Bay (R44).

Cape Point over Ou Kaapse Weg

From Cape Town, you travel the M3 out to Constantia and take the M42 (the Spaanschemat River Road) and choose which of its famous and beautiful estates you'd like to visit: Klein Constantia, Buitenverwachting, Constantia Uitsig or Steenberg. Thereafter, you take the Ou Kaapse Weg road over the pass to the Atlantic side of the peninsula on your way to Cape Point Vineyards, not the southernmost vineyards on the continent, but strikingly different for being where the land moves to an end point – Cape Point. The cellar itself is at the top of the hill where you turn right to go to Kommetjie or left to Fish Hoek; some of the vineyards are on the road just before the turn-off into the Cape Point Nature Reserve with its incredible vistas and pretty lighthouse. Along the way, you can see the seaside villages of Kommetjie and Scarborough, along with beaches that stretch the fittest legs.

The Robertson Road (R60 to R317)

The brochures all talk about the valley of wine and roses, and this valley on the Breede River, centred on the town of Robertson, does offer a big variety for the traveller as well as an environment that is quite different from the conventional vineyard beauty of manicured Stellenbosch. Here the land is drier and sparser, with an open big-sky character that feels liberating. Graham Beck Wines is on your route, then Springfield Estate, Bon Courage and Van Loveren Private Cellar. The side trips offer drives into mini-passes of great beauty: either to quaint Montagu through Ashton with Excelsior, Viljoensdrift and Zandvliet on the way; or the wine-rich areas around Bonnievale, where Quando and Weltevrede are good stops. This is a long trip from Cape Town, so set out early or stay over at one of the many guest houses in the area. For even further travels into the hinterland, take the R62 and stop at the co-operative cellar of Montagu before heading on to the interesting Joubert-Tradauw cellar where good Mediterranean lunches are served in the striking valley. The next town, Barrydale, is a gem, also with a co-op cellar for easy-drinking wines and stickies.

The Modern Architecture Trails

Those who want a new perspective on the ideal of a Cape wine farm should try these breakaways from the whitewash and gable look.

Dornier: Designed by the famed European artist Christoph Dornier to be a winery that blends in with the environment from some angles, while from others it stands proud, this is a fascinating structure that changes according to the phases of the sun. The reflecting pool outside is especially effective in the late afternoons, while the other side creates a playful and multilayered visual effect upon looking back at the roof line with the reflections in the glass. The workings of the winery are also visible through glass walls, and the barrel maturation cellar is a cathedral. The wines are elegant and structured, and there's a good restaurant on the premises.

> Blaauwklippen Road, Stellenbosch
> (021) 880-0557
> Mon-Fri 9am-4.30pm, Sat 9am-2pm

Delaire: This old Stellenbosch favourite has seen a complete revolution under the new ownership of diamond magnate Laurence Graff who has completely refashioned the winery and added a lovely restaurant with an incredible deck to it (see page 139). The tasting room is a magnificent space filled with highbrow art and the grounds are also dotted with sculpture. There is also an arresting new boutique hotel.

> Helshoogte Pass
> (021) 885-1756
> Mon-Sat 10am-5pm

Zorgvliet: In the pretty Banhoek Valley down the road from Tokara, this winery features a tourist-friendly tasting venue with echoes of a game park. The winery itself is an exercise in modern ergonomics, with a viewing deck to observe the inner workings of a most modern facility. Tours by appointment. The wines are very contemporary, soft and well-made; the flagship Zorgvliet label is underpinned by the Silver Myn label of more moderately priced wines. This farm has a great number of activities (horse riding, fly-fishing and a play area for the kids), and a restaurant and coffee shop in the tasting room.

Helshoogte Pass
(021) 885-1399
Mon-Thurs 9am-5pm, Fri to 6pm; Sat 10am-7pm,
Sun 10am-5pm. Visiting times may be more
limited in winter

Waterkloof: Drive off the access road and you'll not see much except vines and the dramatic hills that augur the high Sir Lowry's Pass, but around a few bends and there it is – one of the newest and most arresting wineries of the Cape. It's been designed to be seen from the inside, where the sheets of glass become massive frames for the beautiful landscape and windows show you the winery's inner workings too. A restaurant here is a great place just to stare out at the views (see page 139).

Sir Lowry's Pass Road, Somerset West
(021) 873-2418
Mon-Fri 9am-4.30pm, Sat-Sun 10am-3pm

Graham Beck Wines (Franschhoek and Robertson): The colours may evoke the shades of the earth and the vine, but the structures of these sister wineries are certainly not meant to blend in with the environment. The Robertson winery looks like a Jurassic egg waiting for the return of its sci-fi mother; the Coastal one outside Franschhoek is an exercise in geometric modern art. Both have interesting smaller detail, like ancient doors and sculpture to guard them; inside interesting art also adorns them. The wines are discussed on pages 54-56. They carry a big range of bold and expressive wines – no surprise here – as well as great bubblies.

> Franschhoek: R45 outside Franschhoek
> (021) 874-1258
> Mon-Fri 9am-5pm, Sat 10am-3pm
> Robertson: R60 between Robertson and Worcester
> (023) 626-1214
> Mon-Fri 9am-5pm, Sat 10am-3pm

The Tradition & History Trails

You came to the Cape to see Cape Dutch. Here is a round-up of some of the best examples of this vernacular style that is unique to the Cape, plus a few variations on the theme that are still historically interesting. The Cape Dutch style of architecture is centred around the Heerenhuis (gentleman's house), the formal homestead with its typical gable and thatched roof and white-washed walls. A werf or yard extends out in front of the main house with rows of facing buildings that recede in importance the further away they are. The closest is the Jonkershuis (young man's house) where the son would stay. Some still have the original gardens where the kitchen supplies came from, others the dovecote or mill room.

Groot Constantia Estate: This is the original and still one of the best, a national monument. The layout of the farmstead is traditional and tours through the homestead are offered many times a day at a fee. There's also a museum of old furniture and artefacts, plus an Interpretive Centre for info on the history. Expect it to be a busy experience in summer. The wines are discussed in Grandes Dames (page 18), the range is great and the quality has seen recent improvement. There are two restaurants on the premises, one traditional, one modern – book ahead.

> Constantia Road, Constantia
> (021) 794-5128
> Dec-Apr Mon-Sun 9am-6pm, May-Nov Mon-Sun 9am-5pm

Klein Constantia Estate: The 'smaller' sibling to the above, and certainly less full of bluster (see page 25). For a quieter look at the early Constantia spreads, come here. Tours are by appointment only; this estate also has a very typical layout and is situated in a valley of great beauty. The wines are of good quality; the Sauvignon Blanc is often a stellar wine and the Vin de Constance is a legend, made as the traditional wines of the eighteenth century were.

> Klein Constantia Road
> (021) 794-5188
> Mon-Fri 9am-5pm, Sat 9am-1pm

Vergelegen: Another Grande Dame who is very used to receiving guests and charges her nominal fee at the gate, whereafter a self-guided look around the splendid main homestead, library and magnificent gardens is included. Guided tours are available for an extra fee: 10.30am, 11.30am and 3pm. This is a model Cape farm and all the bits are in the right place with an Interpretive

Centre to add value. The wines are of the Cape's best; see Big Hitters (page 44). Two restaurants are on the premises, also picnics in summer. This is a must-see for a look at history.

Lourensford Road
(021) 847-1334
Mon-Sun 9.30am-4.30pm.

Boschendal Wines: One of the most visitor-friendly and well-maintained estates in the winelands with busloads of happy guests for the wine, the gardens, the picnics and the superb buildings. Tours are offered November through April at 10.30am and 11.30am by appointment and for a fee. The wines are well worth the trip too, see Grande Dames (page 22). Restaurants on the premises, as well as picnics in summer on the lawns – reservations a must.

On the R310 just before the R45 to Franschhoek
(021) 970-4211
Nov-Apr Mon-Sun 8.30am-4.30pm, May-Oct Mon-Sat 8.30am-4.30pm

Uitkyk: The prettiest example of a Georgian manor house in the winelands. Tours are offered by appointment. In 1995, a chance occurrence led to the discovery of beautiful murals in the entrance, hidden under many layers of paint, that depict spring and summer. These are still being restored. The wines are led by the Chardonnay, with a decent Sauvignon Blanc and a few reds to taste too.

R44 between Stellenbosch and Paarl
(021) 884-4416
Mon-Fri 9am-5pm, Sat-Sun 10am-4pm

The Gardens
& Landscapes
Trails

Gardens

A few wine estates have landscaped gardens. In the main these are the ones that date from bygone eras, so they will also offer historic architecture (see Tradition & History Trails page 146). Of these, Vergelegen is particularly notable, if only for the five camphor trees planted in 1700 by W A van der Stel – together these have been declared a national monument. The rest of the estate is a delight too: a formal octagonal garden with a rose garden and a variety of other horticultural delights. Lady Florence Phillips created and restored much of this garden upon becoming the owner in 1917.

> Lourensford Road
> (021) 847-1334
> Mon-Sun 9.30am-4.30pm

Landscapes

Wineries in or near wild and beautiful landscapes give you a real flavour of the local flora – the Cape Floral Kingdom is its own biosphere and the local fynbos (fine or small bush) grows only here. The Cederberg Private Cellar (see page 90) is in the heart of the magnificent Cederberg Mountains, a proclaimed conservation area that's also a natural wilderness area, full of plant and animal life. This winery is placed at the starting point of some superb hiking trails to remarkable mountain rock features, like the Maltese Cross and the Wolfsberg Cracks and Arch. This incredible scenery is not too close – a five-hour round trip from Cape Town – so fortunately the farm also offers straightforward accommodation. This part of the Cape is certainly worth a weekend's visit at the very least.

> **Dwarsrivier Farm. Algeria Road off the N7 to Clanwilliam**
> **(027) 482-2827**
> **Mon-Sat 8am-12.30pm, 2pm-5pm**

Of great historical interest as well as being in the Darling Hills in the heart of the Swartland, an area of great agricultural importance (though historically for maize), is the Groote Post winery. Groote Post means 'big outpost' – historically it was an important trading post and refreshment station for the settlers moving into the interior. This outpost saw some dangerous and lonely times, because colonial expansion was not a soft business – the building that is now the winery was an old fort and today this building and the manor house are national monuments. Also of historic interest is the fact that Hildagonda Duckitt, who wrote one of the earliest Cape cookery books, once lived here. A country kitchen here is named in her honour. The landscapes are open and dramatic, more like a semi-desert and unusual for winelands. But you have sea views from the hills (and cooling breezes) and the soils make good wines. Their Sauvignon Blanc and Chardonnay are worthwhile; the reds are lighter-styled. To explore the surrounds, self-guided walks are a spring delight, when the riotous colours of the wild flowers of the West Coast are in bloom. About a two-hour round trip from Cape Town.

Darling Hills Road off R27 West Coast Road
(022) 492-2825
Mon-Fri 9am-5pm, Sat 9am-3pm

The Arts Trail

The summer season in the winelands is the best time for exploring your arts interests: a few estates have outdoor theatres with music and cultural productions. It's always advisable to reserve for any production, as well as your picnic basket.

Spier rounds out its multi-purpose nature with a grand and comfortable outdoor amphitheatre that plays host to a variety of plays and musical productions in its Summer Arts Festival. For details visit www.spier.co.za

Vergelegen hosts outdoor music events in summer, under the stars with picnic baskets for sale. For details (021) 847-1334.

Paul Cluver's outdoor amphitheatre is a wild and woody affair, a rustic theatre in the midst of a pine forest with wooden tables or embankment seating. Picnic baskets are for sale, or take your own. (021) 844-0605.

Oude Libertas is the cultural centre of Distell, a small outdoors venue with interesting plays and music throughout summer. The restaurant is alongside for an early dinner. www.oudelibertas.co.za

Morgenhof hosts an art exhibition in September in their tasting venue. For details call (021) 889-5510.

Grande Provence has a very good contemporary fine art gallery on the premises. (021) 876-8600.

Glen Carlou is home to some of Donald Hess' international art collection in a dedicated gallery at the tasting room. Modern and big pieces. (021) 875-5528.

Delaire has a permanent collection of local and international art and the gardens feature oversized sculptures. (021) 885-1756.

Steenberg is home to some of Graham Beck's art collection, as well as a selection of his sculptures. (021) 713-2211.

You wouldn't expect Russian art in the Cape winelands, but *Hazendal* interestingly has that, and a collection of Fabergé eggs, too. The small gallery is dedicated to paintings that depict rural Russia, and there's a small icons selection. Another cultural institution, Russian teas, is offered for groups. Call to book (021) 903-5112.

The Curiosities Trail

For a look at things that you wouldn't expect, or those places whose character is most unusual and singular, try these eccentric stops on your travels.

If you want to walk into the past with no guide or sense of careful museum preservation, come and visit *Muratie*. The protected spider webs say it all – this is the most worn-in, wrinkled, moody and eccentric cellar and tasting room you are likely to find; all the crinkles and rough edges of age are celebrated in their natural state. This is actually one of the oldest cellars in the Cape, dating to 1685, and now the space is a strange memorial to both the famous Ronnie Melck, who put the winery back on the map in the twentieth century, and the previous owner and artist, Canitz, whose paintings adorn the gothic lounge. You'll be forgiven for thinking this is the set to some Hollywood folly, like The Addams Family Winery. The first Cape estate to plant Pinot Noir, they still make this as well as a range of other reds and one white, a Chardonnay. The wines are reasonable, the best their Ansela red blend and the Cape Vintage, a port wine.

> **Knorhoek Road, off R44, Stellenbosch**
> **(021) 865-2330**
> **Mon-Fri 9am-5pm, Sat-Sun 10am-4pm**

Another estate that carries the air of history with only a few winds of change blowing through is *Vergenoegd*. The simple working honesty of this very old estate is in direct contrast to the manicured Cape Dutch of most other wineries of similar heritage, and the red wines they make here are similarly old-styled, rather austere but excellent; made for ageing rather than drinking immediately. The wines here seem to be consistently underrated, the estate often forgotten. The reasons why are hard to identify – the wines certainly aren't lacking – but there is something about the aura of the place that makes it feel like it's in a time capsule.

> **R310 to Stellenbosch shortly after turning off N2**

(021) 843-3248
Mon-Fri 8am-4pm, Sat 9.30am-12.30pm

Previously in the heart of Durbanville winelands and now swamped by urban townhouse development is *Altydgedacht*. The boundary between rural and urban is starkly illustrated here. The estate was established in 1698; now the big shopping centre down the road has all the footsoldiers of modern commerce. Time seems to continue to the tick of a different clock here. The Parker family have owned it for five generations and still make good reds, along with another curiosity – Barbera – an Italian grape variety that is very scarce here. Hopefully the winery will outlast the urban onslaught.

Tygerbergvalley Road
(021) 976-1295
Mon-Fri 9am-5pm, Sat 9-1pm

For the most eccentric tour through his own cellar, along with a demonstration of 'sabrage' (opening a bottle of bubbly with a sabre) you must visit *Cabrière Estate* on a Saturday morning for a tour with the winelands' personality, Achim von Arnim. This is the sparkling wine specialist in the Franschhoek valley and Von Arnim is also a specialist in racy humour and bonhomie. Haute Cabrière is the farm's maturation cellar and restaurant on the pass, but the winery is in

Berg Street, Franschhoek
(021) 876-2630
Sat 11am, by appointment weekdays and for groups

The Air, Train & Track Trails

Unusual ways through the winelands for those with a sense of adventure or those who are just tired of driving around.

- Hire a light aeroplane from the Stellenbosch Flying Club if you are a pilot who fancies a look around. (021) 880-0294.
- Helicopter flips are always popular, and you can ask them to drop and collect you from a restaurant. Court Helicopters (021) 425-2966.
- Hot air ballooning is the completely tranquil option. Between November and April you can get a flip over the Paarl region followed by a champagne breakfast at the Grande Roche Hotel. Winelands Ballooning (021) 863-3192.
- Take a ride in an antique train. The Spier Vintage Train goes through the winelands at certain times of the year; check at (021) 419-5222.
- If a horse is your favoured transport, take a trail with Mont Rochelle Equestrian Centre in Franschhoek (021) 876-2362; or the Spier Horse Trails for horse or carriage rides (021) 809-1100.
- For a hike in the hills, try the Helderberg Farm Hiking Trail, with a tea garden that is close to good wine farms for afterwards (021) 855-4308.

- The Jonkershoek Nature Reserve has a number of brilliant walks, and mountain bikes are allowed.
- The Wellington Wine Walk is a four-day affair, from March to November (083) 313-8383. The Green Mountain Trail takes in some spectacular scenery as it traverses mountains and wine farm, including Paul Cluver and Beaumont Wines. Also accommodation en route www.greenmountain.co.za
- A descriptive walk through the wine town of Stellenbosch is also fun and informative. They also do ghost walks ... (021) 887-9150.

The Quick Fix

You are in Cape Town and have little time in hand but want to visit a winery or two. Here are a few solutions – the first for those who have a morning or an afternoon; the second options if you really only have time for one, but want to get the whole winelands experience – buildings, scenery and wine.

'I've got half a day'

The Constantia Route: M42 off the M3 highway to Muizenberg

For the perfect introduction to the region, this area is the classic half-day visit. The places are exceedingly pretty and well-mannered, and they exude genteel charm. Try them in this order:

- First go to the furthest, Steenberg, to taste their Sauvignon Blancs and Sémillon – they'll knock your socks off. It has a bit of a grandiose, corporate feeling – and an expensive golf course if you have the inclination and can find the time ...
- Next stop is Buitenverwachting for some great Chardonnay and lovely red wines in a more restrained style (page 26).
- Then mosey further down the same road to Klein Constantia Estate for some more reds (if you still have the need) but mainly for one of the best dessert wines around (see page 25).
- If you've only got time for lunch now, go to nearby Constantia Uitsig; or press on to the nearby Groot Constantia Estate (page 18) for a look around one of the icons of the Cape (but be aware that this can take some time – this estate is also a one-stop if you are really pressed for time). You can lunch here too.

The Durbanville Route: Head for the M13 off the R31 from the N1 north

This is a lovely, balanced route, with some traditional wineries and others that are much more in the New World style. You will also get to see beautiful views from the top of the Durbanville Hills of the Atlantic Ocean and of Table Mountain.

- Begin at Altydgedacht, a very old cellar with bags of charm. They are best known for their reds, but make a few lovely whites, including a floral Gewürztraminer.

- The next stop along the road is Bloemendal, where you will find a super Sauvignon Blanc and Sémillon; ditto at the following winery Nitida, so you can do a comparative tasting. Both these estates have some good reds too; Bloemendal, a Shiraz and Nitida, a Cabernet Sauvignon and Pinotage.
- The final stop is on top of Durbanville Hills at the cellar of the same name, a modern edifice with a selection of easy-drinking wines at good prices. The views here are superb, and you can capitalise on them by having lunch here.

'I've only got time for one'

Choose from these one-stop wonders:
- Groot Constantia Estate has it all: the traditional buildings, the gardens, the views and the restaurants – as well as a range of wines that is constantly improving. The fact that you can have a look through the Heerenhuis is a plus, making this the ideal in close-by tourist attractions. (See page 18 for more.) 20 minutes from Cape Town.
- Spier in Stellenbosch is the ultimate all-round entertainer for the whole family: wine, food, gardens, music, animals. The Moyo restaurant on the premises is an entertainment in itself with African dance and music. But don't be lulled into thinking that the wines are light-weight. See page 57. 30 minutes from Cape

Town.

- Fairview's tasting room is so well organised and their all-round offering so good that this is an ideal one-stop. Great wines, excellent cheeses, goats for the kids to gawk at, and a restaurant on site. See page 65. 40 minutes from Cape Town.

THE FAQs OF WINE

What is good wine?

The million-dollar question. This question has launched a thousand wine competitions, but none of the results seem to correlate, which doesn't really help us. Your friends have their opinions; you have a few of your own. Can we get to the truth of the matter? The truth is: Wine and its greatness are largely relative.

But while great may be relative, good and poor are easier to tell apart. A good wine has certain hallmarks. Synchronicity is the first. There should be a correlation between what you smell on the nose and what you taste. Then, in the mouth, you are searching for balance. The harmony between fruit, acid and tannin on the palate. Most pundits agree that balance marks good wine. Finally you assess length. A good wine lasts in the mouth, lingering pleasantly. It remains good to drink the whole way through the bottle; and doesn't become cloying, or astringent, or simply disappear. Perhaps the sternest test comes next: Is the wine likeable enough to finish – not just a glass, but the whole bottle? And then – do you wish you had another?

One caveat is that wine will perform very differently in different situations, with different food, places and people; so you need, more or less, the right wine for the occasion.

Carrie Adams of specialist wine shop Norman Goodfellows, Illovo, has this take on it:

+ **What are the hallmarks of good wine?**

'They should be good and clean and fresh. There are too many dirty, tainted wines around. You need to smell and taste and go with your gut – is this fresh wine?'

+ **What are you looking for when you sniff?**

'On red wines, berries and red and black fruit pastilles. On whites, the yellow and orange fruit pastilles. You want to smell the fruit!'

+ **What are you looking for on the palate?**

'The same as what you've smelt, so you want accord. Then, you want the wine to fill your mouth – you don't want a mean and tight wine, it should be Rubensesque!'

How does one taste wine?

Tasting wine in a technical fashion (for assessment) and drinking wine are two different pursuits and should never be confused. Wine tasting is a technical/comparative exercise to discuss and analyse wines and to get to know them better. Drinking wine on the other hand is clearly all about enjoyment. If you are visiting a few wineries for comparative purposes and to decide what you want to buy, these are the basics:

• Swirl the glass to release the volatile aromas and take a sniff at the top of the glass – what do you smell? And, more importantly, do you like what you smell?

- Take a sip. Again, you should enjoy the wine; in addition, a good wine has some congruence between what you smelt and what you now taste. If this is a really good wine, there should be balance and length in the mouth. A new vintage red may have too much tannin (they pucker the mouth); take into account that these will soften with a bit of age, or with some food. It's important to imagine what this wine was made for – is it a wine to drink as an apéritif, or was it made to go with food?

- And always remember – really to get to know a wine, you have to spend some time with it. One winemaker calls it 'emotional time'. A wine will develop and improve as it stands in your glass.

What is the point of vintage?

It's amazing how a product as time-bound as wine can so often be presented with no regard for its age. If a dog ages seven years for every one of ours, it would have to be said that the average Cape red ages five to eight years for every human year. Like a human, a wine is most boisterous and crass in youth, at its most accomplished in its middle years, and generous, forgiving and wise in age, when it is often also the most interesting. Age does count.

A wine's vintage year is also like its zodiac sign (only it's more accurate than any human horoscope). The vintage year – whether it was hot or cool, wet or dry in various combinations – will foretell a great deal about the wine's potential for development.

Many wines are drunk very early in their development, in their infancy, and the drinker will never know what they could have become. With this trend, our appreciation and knowledge of wine sticks at a pre-pubescent level, where we enjoy most of our interaction. Vintage has little chance to express itself, so that the wine's character is based almost purely on generic values – the character of being simply a Cabernet, or a Shiraz and not necessarily a complex wine.

It is true to say that many wines are now being made to be generic – and not individuals – they are engineered to be enjoyed straight off the shelf. Yet almost all wines will improve in the bottle, which is why wine is a more ephemeral, time-bound (and for this reason more fascinating) drink than beer, cola or spirits. The vintage says a great deal about a wine's individual character, and is the countervailing spirit to the concept of wine as commodity, all uniform and as alike as possible.

So when should I drink my wine?

Rules of thumb for Cape wines:
- Most whites (unwooded), within two years. Riesling, being an exception, within ten years.
- Wooded Chardonnay, within five years.
- Light reds (little oak), within three years.
- Full-bodied reds, within eight to ten years.
- Sweet wines you can keep for ten years or more, some for decades.

How should I keep my wines?

Lying on their sides in a dedicated cellar at about 14-16°C and 80 per cent humidity with no light is the perfect answer.

We don't all live with access to such conditions, so you have to replicate them as closely as possible. The main factors are to avoid sudden changes in temperature and to leave the bottles on their sides in a cool place. A wine will age more quickly in a warm area – important to note if you are out in the winelands on a hot day. The boot of a car is hell for wine, and can destroy them, so keep your movements swift! Of course, few people seem interested in cellaring wines these days: they generally buy and drink them almost immediately – in this case, it's important to serve your wines at the right temperature.

Why is temperature important for serving wine?

Much of what makes wine special and gives it its character are compounds that the nose picks up and translates into taste. These compounds need to be delivered to the olfactory system at the right temperature for optimal pick-up. That's around 18-20°C for red wines and 12-14°C for whites. At very low temperatures, they aren't given a chance to express themselves, and remain mute.

If the temperature is too high, the volatile aromas just blow off and disappear. Practically, for reds, the wine must be cool, never summer 'room' temperature because that would be too hot. For whites, not refrigerator cold, but distinctly cool enough for the bottle to condensate. Bubblies and sweet wines need to be even colder than that.

Should I open my red wine ahead of time to let it breathe?

The idea behind letting a wine breathe is to put it into contact with oxygen to begin the processes that liberate the wine's smells and flavours. If you pull the cork and leave the bottle, precious little of the wine is in contact with oxygen. You need to decant the wine into a decanter or simply a jug and really get some air in there. This will make even the most modest red wine immeasurably better.

The only exception is a very old red. Like any aged thing, they don't like too much action. These wines should not be decanted, because their structure is delicate and ephemeral, and decanting can do more harm than good. Pour these delicately from the bottle, and take care not to pour out the natural deposits that are likely to sit at the bottom of the bottle.

Is the shape of the glass really important?

It may seem pretentious and wine snobby, but the shape of the glass is vital to wine enjoyment. You can do the experiment yourself by pouring wine into a tumbler, a goblet (open) wine glass, and a tulip-shaped glass. Smell and taste the wine and see if they seem to be the same wine. The shape actually affects the smell and therefore the taste of wine. As a start point, the tulip shape (e.g. a tasting glass) is important, as it funnels the aroma to your nose (the most important organ in wine tasting). In general, white wines benefit from narrower shapes (but not smaller); while reds like bigger bowls at the base. Bespoke glassware from companies like Riedel and Spiegelau manufacture a glass for almost every variety of wine and claim they enhance that specific grape. Varietal wines do indeed taste uniquely good in these glasses, and do change in taste from shape to shape, so there's something to it – and they've done intensive research! Besides which, a good glass simply looks so much better on the table.

How do I know which wine to put with which food?

A great deal is written about wine and food matching and a pretentious air has settled on the supposedly arcane knowledge of what goes with what. It's very simple, really, once you decide philosophically to go beyond the point of 'I drink what I like when I like' – which is a valid position. The everyday reality is that we typically open only one or two bottles to go with everyone's whole meal – not a wine with every course, and certainly not catering to everyone's individual choice.

Assuming that there is the opportunity to do some matching, these are the basic, broad concepts to use: match weight to weight, texture to texture and sweetness to sweetness. It's all about matching the tannins, the acidity and the sweetness. The safest pairings are usually those where the wines are closest to the food in character. In other words, big and rich (Cabernet) will work with steak. The old rule of red meat with red wine, and white with white, is a broad and safe bet, but you could miss out on some interesting matches – and one of the most important pairing concepts is to look at your dominant flavour ... this is often in the sauce that covers the (red or white) meat. Veal in a creamy sauce will obviously go better with a rich white than the red that veal on its own would suggest.

So, if your food is light with delicate, fresh textures, move into the light, delicate whites like bubblies, unwooded Chenins and dry Gewürztraminers.

If it's mixed, like antipasti, with colour, flavour and substance, you need a fruity red like a young Cabernet, young, light Shiraz, a Pinotage or a dry rosé. A flavoursome white like Riesling will also work.

If it's rich seafood and especially shellfish, go with a wooded Chardonnay. If the seafood is especially oily (snoek or sardine), try Riesling; and if it has been char-grilled, remember that the flavour will turn to the smoke – go with a light Merlot.

A hamburger or a simple meat dish will also suit a Merlot or a Shiraz; if you are doing some dedicated outdoor grilling, go with big-hearted Shiraz.

Pasta always depends on the sauce – if it is tomato-based, try a lighter Cabernet Sauvignon or red blend; if it is creamy, go with a rich Chardonnay. If it is both, stick to the red (the acids of tomato will kill the Chardonnay). Ditto for pizza: the tomato and toppings are crying out for some tannins.

There are some enduring classic match-ups:

- Cabernet Sauvignon with steak
- Pinot Noir with lamb
- Sauvignon Blanc with asparagus, and also white fish
- Bubbly with oysters
- Dessert wine with foie gras (as long as it has enough acidity)

There are also some that are classically misunderstood:

- Cheese on its own often does not go well with red wine (it's too tannic); rather try a rich white like Chardonnay
- Eggs murder wine, and, no matter what anyone says, spicy Indian food goes better with beer
- Sweet wines must be 'bigger' than the dessert to work, therefore sweeter or more acidic to cut through the richness. Chocolate is a dry wine killer, so opt for port or muscadel instead

Unusual matches can really work, try sushi with lighter reds (Pinotage is a winner) or sashimi with a natural sweet wine.

After all is debated, the single most important rule is: *Wine is generally more delicate in structure than food, so, if in doubt, make the wine the bigger of the two, or tone the food's flavour down. Give the wine a fair chance!*

And the second most important rule: *If in doubt, serve dry bubbly. At least everyone will be in a party mood.*

When can I send a wine back in a restaurant?

- When the wine is 'corked'. This happens when a chemical compound (2,4,6-trichloroanisole or TCA) gets out of hand and spoils the smell and taste of the wine – it will have a mildly off-putting smell that some people associate with wet cardboard, others with mousiness. It does not go away when you swirl the glass, as some other 'pongs' can. The wine is likely to have little taste if it is afflicted with TCA.
- When the wine tastes baked, or oxidised. What this means is that the wine has been stored badly or the cork leaked. The wine tastes thin and vinegary and has a 'hot' rusty smell with a dull taste.

  - Note that many restaurants have a very bad habit of over-filling the wine glass. A glass that's over half full is over full. Try to prevent this – it means that you can't get a good whiff of those wonderful aromas.

Are screwcaps okay?

This is an ongoing debate, but the answer has to be yes.

Screwcaps are the ultimate closure in that they do not let in any air if they seal properly. This is the ideal condition in which to preserve the wine as the winemaker meant it to be. Screwcaps are becoming more and more popular and ultimately they are likely to seal most of the wine we drink. But screwcaps don't have the romance, or the luscious 'pop' that suggests the good times are about to roll. That's why screwcaps are more accepted with easy drinking wines. But more and more 'serious' wines are beginning to use them. After all is said and done, it's a monumental shame when a wine that's had years of care put into it is spoilt by a bad piece of tree hide.

On the other hand, the screwcap, since it's fully manufactured, has more of a 'carbon footprint' than the naturally renewable cork, and the cork manufacturers are working hard to fix the problems with TCA compounds (which cause a wine to be 'corked') so who knows where this battle will end. It's also important to remember that you must still smell and taste a wine under screwcap the same way you do for a wine under cork, because TCA could have crept into the wine from an earlier source in the cellar, so a wine can still be 'corked' even though the bottle has a screwcap.

Do those gold stickers on the bottle mean much?

Wine competitions are like lotteries – the more of them an estate enters, the more likely it is that it will win someday. A gold award does mean a panel of experts deem the wine of superior quality (only against the other entrants), so if you are in unknown territory with rows and rows in front of you, it can be of some reassurance. But it's good to be aware that some styles of wine are more likely to do well at competitions – wines that have the most gregarious personalities always stand out.

The shyer, perhaps more complex, wines are often overlooked. Then there is the subjectivity of wine panels: the same wine that wins a gold award in one may bomb out in another. In fact, a recent study undertaken by Robert Hodgson and published in the Journal of Wine Economics revealed that in the case of 4 000 wines entered for 13 wine competitions in the USA, there was almost no consensus in the results. Wines receiving gold medals in one or more competitions would very often not even receive a mention in any of the others. His summary was that the likelihood of winning a gold medal can only be explained by chance! So competitions and gold stickers are certainly no guarantee that you will like the wine, but they generally seem to impress at most dinner parties.

Icons, cult and first growth. What is a status wine?

The competitiveness of the wine industry and the natural desire for market share leads to the fight for status, and the establishment of tiers of importance. Aside from ego gratification, an estate's position on a rung clearly has useful marketing and sales implications. In France, wine areas within regions have been classified, over time, into codified ranks of importance. The idea is that certain areas are better than others for grape production, proven by certain producers who have historically excelled. In the Bordeaux region, the highest on the ladder are called First Growths: with fewer than ten of them, this is a highly significant title.

Here, in South Africa, we don't have any official categories of superiority, so the producers duke it out, often claiming status for themselves as making 'first growth,' 'icon,' or 'cult' wine. Of the three, 'cult' is the outlier, implying a wine of less mainstream demand, and recognition only with those in the know. An 'icon' wine is one that everyone should know, and is sure to come at a high price.

While status is a matter of opinion here, it's becoming clear that a track record of excellence is a prerequisite, and it's generally assumed that ten years is the absolute minimum by which to judge consistent excellence in wine.

What's up with 'New World' and 'Old World'?

As simple as the geographic distinction between Europe (the Old World) and the countries that once were colonies (the New), this distinction takes on a broader meaning in winespeak. It is used to differentiate between two philosophies of winemaking, two approaches – though, as time goes by, the differences are being eroded by cross-pollination, the one borrowing the strengths of the other.

Old World winemaking is defined by tradition. Wine is made in the same places, in the same way and in the same style as it always was. Nature is the key factor in deciding on the course of the wine, and yearly climatic variations (with concomitant variations in quality) are accepted and even celebrated as expressive of nature. Wines are primarily about expressing terroir (see the next question), and may often consist of blends of grapes. The varieties of grapes themselves are not the main attraction.

New World is defined by progress. New ways of making wines, novel cellar technique, experimentation in process and the exploration of uncharted areas are par for the course. In many instances, there just isn't the centuries-long track record that Europe has. Nature is more likely to be manipulated by high tech vineyard management and cellar technology to create wines that are always consistent in quality. Wine is defined by variety and expressing the flavours of the particular fruit is paramount.

Clearly, each can learn from the other, and, in a New World like ours, the best wines are made with respect for both approaches.

What is meant by the term terroir?

Sometimes there is a French word for a concept that we can only describe in an English paragraph (like this below). One such word is 'terroir'. It literally means terrain, but in winemaking terms it means a whole lot more. Terroir is the combination of a variety of elements that make up the growing conditions of the vine. The soil is key, as is the aspect or slope, the macro- and the microclimate, winds, rainfall, etc. They are unique and absolutely local elements – the power of place. These factors are beyond human control. You either have good terroir for winemaking, or you grow broccoli. But a key part of terroir is also the human element: the philosophical (and scientific) approach of the viticulturist. As we know, humans can improve or hopelessly misuse what nature provides. The term terroir contains all of these things: it is the combination of all the forces that have shaped the vine, so it's a pretty cool word to bandy about. We hand it to the French, but then they did have to borrow 'weekend' from us.

What's the deal with organic wines?

Organic sounds good. We like the earth. But organic wine should be as good to drink as it is to think. We feel better about drinking it because it's better for the environment – but, crucially, it should also taste good, otherwise we are simply martyrs to the cause. So, does it?

Let's begin with a look at what organic is all about. You get conventional wine, organic wine and finally bio-dynamic wine. They move along a continuum based on how much intervention there is in the winemaking process. Conventional winemaking utilises any available route to maximum quality and ideal volume at best prices. Employing chemically synthesised fertilisers, pesticides and herbicides, they create the easiest growing conditions for the vine. The aim is fruit that is consistent, unspoilt, bountiful – but potentially uniform and undifferentiated, a shiraz from South Africa tasting more and more like one from Australia. Plus the volume of chemicals needed to keep the vineyards performing at their peak just keep rising, as the bugs become resistant and the soils are stripped of their own nutrients.

The organic wine producer chooses to avoid this cul-de-sac. The buzzword is sustainability, with an emphasis on good husbandry and less intervention. Vines are grown without the use of strong chemical compounds, composts are used instead. Soft intervention is practised in the vineyard, like encouraging natural predators to remove pests – ladybirds to remove mealy bug, squadrons of ducks to devour snails. One of the chief differences between a conventional and an organic vineyard is the presence of insect and animal life in the rows of plants. It takes up to seven years for a vineyard that was conventional to be given organic status – which status is monitored and certified by various organisations.

Then you get bio-dynamic. This is a step beyond organic, but the logical extension of it. Rooted in the writings of Rudolf Steiner, it's a return to very traditional farming, allied to a harmonious outlook on the world and one's own place in it. It differs from organic in three respects: bio-dynamic farms are mixed farms, based on the observation that monocultures do not exist in nature; secondly, they use traditional herbal preparations such as those found in the books of the English botanist Culpeper to add vitality to the soils; and, thirdly, they farm according to the lunar cycle. Bio-dynamic farming has an integrated, non-interventionist approach, completely at odds with conventional farming. For example, pests and weeds are considered natural, as long as they don't dominate. Their mantra is 'stability through diversity'. We have a few bio-dynamic producers in the Cape, for example Reyneke and Mountain Oaks, and many more are beginning to produce organic wines.

This is all good and well, but the pressing question remains: does organic wine taste as good as conventional wine? The short answer is some do and some don't – just like any selection of wine is variable. It is hard to resist the feeling that they have a distinctly 'earthy' flavour, but this may just be the connotation. So you just have to go ahead and taste them, and if you like, you can add their happy philosophy to your pleasure of them.

What makes some wine cost more?

Wine is a high-end agricultural product, and the bottle is the result of at least five years of many people's hard work – and not inconsiderable capital. So a really cheap wine has to be really ordinary, bulk wine (sometimes even imported from countries where the costs of manufacturing are lower).

All wine starts as a grape, which costs more to grow the more you care for it, the first step to an expensive wine. All wines have the foundation costs of acquiring a prime piece of land, preferably with all the right adjectives attached – cool climate, sea breezes, soils of the right composition, etc. (These help the marketing as well as the quality.) Then you have to carry the farming costs of planting the vines, growing the grapes and harvesting them, then making the wine and putting it into a bottle. This is the really unglamorous stuff, the kind of work that should be well compensated. These are the baseline costs, including the expense of running the winery. Arguably, these costs are relatively even across all wines, unless a state of the art winery is being set up and the wines are defraying this. Looking at only these issues, bottled white wine costs should be within R20 of each other.

From picking, the way the grape is further treated is pertinent to price. Hand-sorted? Fermented in stainless steel or wood? Matured for 12 months or 18? Bottle matured on the farm? Bottled in big, heavy glass or in a bag? Well marketed and advertised or bottom of shelf? Most white wine, as a case in point, is lower priced because of the significant impact that the cost of new French oak barrels (used to mature reds) has.

However, some whites carry the additional production costs of having been fermented and/or matured in oak barrels. When you talk French oak barrels (which most winemakers like to talk) you are spending many thousands of rands extra every time the word 'barrique' is casually mentioned. This is the most obvious reason why a Chardonnay will cost more than a Sauvignon Blanc, because it's more often the convention to put some oak on to Chardonnay.

But then the more slippery, variable costs begin to impact. Like: not all grapes are equal. Chardonnay is 'more equal' than Riesling, for example. Sauvignon Blanc is 'more equal' than Chenin Blanc. Why? Fashion. Different grape varieties obviously make different tasting wines, with different styles. Riesling used to be fashionable, now Sauvignon Blanc rules, but Riesling may come back into mode. Everyone still loves Chardonnay; it's like the blue jeans of wine. Fashion is crucial to desirability: it influences demand, the price of the grape and the finished wine. (Sauvignon Blanc has been the craze for a good few years now, a fresh, brash (arguably), undemanding wine that suits the prevailing casual lifestyle – hence its higher price.)

Then there is the historic perception that some varieties make better wines than others, and have more character or a character that should be taken more seriously. Chardonnay refers: this more intellectual white (especially when put into wood) is the acme, easily the highest priced dry white wine.

Lastly, add the style, approach, attitude and reputation of the winery – a 'famous' brand may well turn that into a higher sticker price. And all the marketing costs to help convince us to take the wine off the shelf ... these can all rack up a good few extra digits.

What additives are found in wine?

While wine is by and large a natural product, the finished bottle usually contains sulphites in controlled amounts. Interestingly, these levels are usually lower than those you will find in your average fruit juice, so if you can drink guava juice just fine, you should have no 'allergy' to wine.

Sulphur is used as a preservative, to scavenge any oxygen that will prematurely age the wine. There is now a trend to reduce the sulphur content of wine through better cellar practice. Any other additives, like flavourants, are strictly illegal (and universally despised) in the South African wine industry.

BUYING WINE

The Wine Specialist

Vaughn Johnson's been selling wine in Cape Town's V&A Waterfront since the mid-1980s. I asked him some questions about buying wine.

What's the role of a wine shop now that every supermarket's got wine?

Good old-fashioned personal service cannot be replaced. In an era of impersonal supermarket shopping in a rushed and frantic world, we forget that shopping can be fun – and a pleasant social activity. Wine has so much of a story but it's often shrouded in mystery or jargon, so there's a need for friendly, professional advice. We don't sell alcohol, we sell stories. Also, with over 7000 South African wines to choose from, a good shop offers you a decent cross-section of worthwhile wines – and at all price points. Because we speak to our customers, we can also respond to what they are looking for and source unusual or scarce wines.

Do you need to spend a lot to get a good wine?

There's real value in South African wines in the under R100 category. One doesn't always get R100 more quality for a R200 spend. There's a grey area between R100-R200 where wannabees and new producers try to recoup costs.

What about bargain bin wines?

This is a good time for the consumer, because there's a lot of wine around, and one of South Africa's greatest strengths is our enormous value at all price points. So our entry level wines are often very good value – but you need the right introduction. Again this is where a specialist shop gives you the personal introduction.

What makes for a 'blue chip' wine?

Proven track record of consistent high quality. Great examples would be De Toren's Fusion V, Rustenberg's Peter Barlow and Kanonkop's Paul Sauer.

How do you feel about restaurant wine prices?

There's no justification for the 300-400 per cent mark-ups in places where the wine is often bought on Monday and sold on Thursday. A wine shop marks up by 30-40 per cent, offers a discount by the case, runs an account and delivers. Then there's the pernicious practice of listing fees where producers have to pay to be on certain restaurant's wine lists. This kills choice and hurts the little guy who can't compete.

Virtual Shopping

Online shopping makes a lot of sense when it comes to wine, because a few cases of wine is a drag to move around and because you can often make a selection from a wide variety, with notes on the wine to help your purchase. Well-established online sites have excellent courier services that make sure the wine arrives in good condition, at their risk. It is worth keeping in mind that these are also shop fronts, and they will have their own favourites and incentives to sell certain labels, but if you see wines you like, it's a great option. They will also be a little more expensive than buying from a conventional shop due to transport costs. Surf these sites:

- www.cybercellar.com
- www.ewine.co.za
- www.winesense.co.za

How to get the most from any restaurant's wine list

The ritual of opening the wine list and languorously considering its delights should be a wonderful part of dining out. A good selection, pertinent descriptions, perhaps a sommelier to help you decide … that's the fantasy we subscribe to – but is this the reality?

In reality the wine list is often either disappointing or daunting. On the disappointing end, what's interesting is how often wine lists in restaurants give the lie to the suggestions of quality that the eatery is trying to convince you of. A great location, money spent on fine fittings, a menu that boasts fresh this and the best that, seasonal treats – and a wine list that is built on average and very commercial wines, heftily marked up. These are the majority of wine lists, made up solely of big brands and showing a complete lack of imagination when it comes to wine, or a simple lack of interest. They sell what sells automatically, and don't want to take any vinous risks. This is most glaring when contrasted with a menu that dazzles with culinary delight. The wine list shows the establishment's real breeding. A danger sign is a wine list full of misspellings – if it's here, such indifference to detail is likely to be present elsewhere.

Then there's the daunting list. We've all come across them – so many unknown wines and no sommelier to help. Remember these tips for everyday wine list success. (Of course, if you are only out to impress, you need look no further than the right-hand column on any list.)

• Avoid the wine by the glass

It's lovely when a list has a number of wines by the glass, but when there is only one white and one red, you are strongly advised to order a bottle of something else. And when there are a number of offerings by the glass, check yours for freshness. A stale wine will smell rusty, it's been standing around open for too long.

• Order from the middle

The mid-point of the price range is often where the quality-value curves meet, so choose the style of wine you are after, and plump for the mid-priced one.

• Pick a blended wine

The Cape has a Mediterranean climate which is best suited (due to its moderate character) to blends. As a rule, extreme climates make good single variety wines (think of the cold Rhinegau) while in moderate climes complexity has to be 'built' through clever blends. So blends are often the better wines on any list, and this is also true for white wines.

- Skip Sauvignon Blanc

Unless you simply have to have it, Sauvignon Blanc is usually overpriced because it's such a fashionable item. If you want a fresh white wine, try a Chenin Blanc or a Riesling where you are likely to find better value and more personality for your rand.

- Understand the reserve list

A good restaurant should cellar wines and then release them at their optimal age. You will pay dearly for this, but it can be worth it. Where the reserve list should be eyed with suspicion is when the wines are not from an old vintage. In this case, the wines simply carry an even higher mark-up and you are often paying for brand. Of course, you may want to pay for brand if the object is conspicuous consumption.

- If in doubt, stick to the basics

There will inevitably be some wines you know and you're better off with something you're sure about instead of delving into the unknown. Dining should not be frustrating; it's bad for the digestion. Wines like Buitenverwachting Blanc and Beyerskloof Pinotage are like salt and pepper, they're in pretty much every restaurant and you can always rely on them.

WINE RULES

Selecting wine

1. Visit a specialist: A good wine shop will have made a pre-selection for you, plus they can recommend something personally. (See page 177.) If you know what you want, e-retail is a great option.
2. Know the occasion: Consider the environment you'll be in – the type of food, the time of day and the company. Match lighter wines or richer wines or prestige wines accordingly.
3. If you want a light, crisp white, go with a screwcap wine for freshness.
4. If you want the best value in your red, go with a blended wine, they're good in the budget range and great at the top end too.
5. If you want something better, remember that there are very few really good whites below R50 or reds below R80.

Enjoying wine

6. Don't just pull the cork half an hour before drinking to let it 'breathe'. A wine only breathes when it has been opened for many hours or when it's vigorously decanted.
7. White can work with red meats and vice versa. Match the texture and weight of your food to the wine. So seared tuna

is fish, but it's actually pretty red with a meaty texture – it will go fine with a light red like a Pinot Noir or a Merlot.

8. Very few cheeses work with reds (Parmesan is one that does). Most cheese, being soft and creamy, clashes with the tannin in red wine. Rather try creamy cheese with Chardonnay or goat's cheese with Sauvignon Blanc.

9. Forget room temperature. This concept is borrowed from eighteenth century Europe, where the rooms were a good deal cooler than they are today. Ours are often positively warm. No wine should be served over 18°C, and whites cooler than that.

10. Colour tells you very little about innate wine quality. A darker wine is not more concentrated in anything except colour and some wines of great complexity are very light, like Pinot Noir.

11. Unless you're setting a formal table, one wine glass fits all. Whites actually taste better served in bigger red wine glasses, so simply use one, good glass. Good means tulip-shaped, with a biggish bowl.

12. Blended wines are often the best wines. Forget the idea that blends are simply what they had left over (unless you are shopping for bargain wine). At the top end, blends are greater than the sum of the parts and the art of the blend is the winemaker's finest achievement.

13. 'Soetes' (sweet wines) can be stellar. Our Cape sweet wines, often called 'dessert' wines, are some of the best in the world. Just don't drink them with dessert! They are dessert on their own, or great as a (well-chilled) aperitif. Then there's the blue cheese match …

14. Appreciate wine in a food context. A tangy, tannic red? Put it with a steak and watch it come alive. A bright, acidic white? Difficult to drink on its own, but alongside your linefish? Superb. Pretty much any wine improves with food.

THE JARGON

In your travels, you may encounter a few terms that you don't know (wine is full of technical terminology). While wine appreciation does not absolutely depend on them, the main terms are explained here to help you if you're doing a quiz or want to silence a dinner party.

Accessible, approachable: When wine flavours are harmonious; a wine that is ready to drink.

Acetic acid: The acid that gives vinegar its characteristic taste. Small amounts are normal in wine; larger amounts give wine a vinegar-like character.

Acidity: Gives wine its crispness. Grapes have two primary acids: tartaric and malic. In South Africa, winemakers are allowed to add acid.

Aftertaste: The lingering flavours of a wine; its persistence. A long aftertaste is a good characteristic.

Alcohol: Produced when yeasts ferment the sugars in the grape. Alcohol gives an impression of fullness, richness and, at higher levels, sweetness. Also a preservative, helping to keep wines in good condition. Measured by volume of the total liquid.

Alluvial: Soil that contains clay, silt, sand or gravel deposited by running water is alluvial. Grapes grown in mostly sandy and stony alluvial soil produce wines with more concentrated fruit flavours.

Aroma: The fragrance of the wine when sniffed.

Astringent: A mouth-puckering sensation associated with high tannin levels (and sometimes acid).

Attack: Initial sensations on palate or nose.

Backbone: A wine with structure, not flabby or insipid. This is often from acid or tannin content.

Baked: 'Hot', earthy quality. Usually from scorched grapes, or from too warm a barrel fermentation, especially in some whites.

Balance: When the wine's components – alcohol, acid, tannin, fruit and wood (where used) – are in harmony.

Barrel ageing: Leaving wine in oak barrels to allow flavour and aromatic compounds to develop.

Barrel character: The flavour and aromatic compounds that an oak barrel contributes to the wine. Barrel character varies by the type of wood, coopering techniques including toasting and length of oak ageing, and the age of the barrel.

Barrel fermentation: The conversion of grape juice into wine by yeast in an oak barrel. Barrel fermentation gives wines complexity and integrated oak flavour.

Bead/Mousse: Bubbles in sparkling wine; a fine, long-lasting bead is the most desirable.

Bitter: Sensation often perceived in the finish of a wine. Sometimes more positively associated with the taste of a specific fruit or nut, such as cherry-pip or almond.

Blend: A wine made from two or more different grape varieties, vintages, vineyards or containers. Some of the world's finest wines are blends.

Bloom: Flowering of the grapevines. Bloom is also a waxy substance found on the skins of grapes.

Body: A sensation of fullness on the palate.

Bottle-age: The development of aromas/flavours (i.e. complexity) as wine matures after bottling. As a negative, bottle-age means a wine with stale, empty, or even off odours.

Botrytis: Caused by a fungus that attacks ripe grapes. The benevolent form is known as 'noble rot' which is responsible for the world's finest sweet wines.

Brix/Balling: The measurement of soluble solids in grapes at harvest, taken with a refractometer and expressed in degrees. In unfermented grapes, degrees of Brix are approximately the same as the percentage of sugar. After fermentation, the alcohol concentration is roughly half the sugar concentration of the juice. Thus, grapes harvested at 22.5 degrees Brix will produce a wine with an alcohol content between 12.5 to 13.5 per cent.

Bud: A small protuberance on a stem or branch, often enclosed in protective scales and containing an undeveloped shoot, leaves or flowers.

Bud break: When the first shoots emerge on a vine after winter dormancy.

Buttery: Flavour and texture associated with barrel-fermented white wines, especially Chardonnays; a rich, creamy smoothness.

Cane: The previous season's shoots that have matured and become woody. Selected canes are retained in some styles of pruning for the following season's fruit production.

Canopy: The leaves and shoots of grapevines.

Cap: The grape skins that float to the top of fermenting red wines, forming a 'cap'.

Carbonic maceration: Method of fermenting wine without crushing grapes first. Whole clusters with stalks, etc are put into closed vat; fermentation occurs within the grape berries, which then burst.

Chaptalisation: A French term for the addition of sugar to grape must to raise the alcohol levels. Not permitted in South Africa.

Charmat method: Method of making sparkling wine in a sealed tank (cuvée close) under pressure. Easier, cheaper than méthode champenoise.

Clarify: Refers to the winemaking operation which removes lees (dead yeast cells and fragments of grape skins, stems, seeds and pulp) from grape juice or new wine.

Clone: A subgroup within a variety of genetically identical plants propagated from a single vine to perpetuate selected or special characteristics.

Cold soak: Cold maceration. Red winemaking method carried out prior to alcoholic fermentation. Skins and juice of red grapes are held, usually for a few days, at a sufficiently cool temperature to prevent fermentation. Supposed to extract flavours gently.

Cold stabilisation: A technique of chilling wines before bottling to cause the precipitation of harmless tartrate crystals.

Complexity: The term used when a wine has multiple flavour and aroma characteristics from the vineyard source, winemaking techniques and/or bottle development.

Corky/Corked: An 'off' characteristic in wines due to a chemical compound, trichloroanisole or TCA. A 'corked' wine cannot always be detected by smelling the cork, the wine must be smelled. TCA diminishes the fruit character of the wine, substituting a character like mouldy newspapers or old swimming pool towels.

Creamy: A silky, buttery feel and texture in wine.

Crisp: Refers to acidity. Positively: means fresh, clean; negatively: too tart, sharp.

Deep and depth: Having many layers; intense; describes a serious wine.

Dense: Well-padded texture, flavour-packed.

Diatomaceous earth: A light, brittle material derived from fossilised microscopic unicellular algae called diatoms, used as a filter in clarifying wine.

Dosage: The sugar added to méthode champenoise or Méthode Cap Classique (MCC) after the second fermentation.

Dry: The absence of a sweet taste sensation.

Dry-fermented: Wine that is fermented until it is dry, meaning that all the sugar is converted to alcohol and carbon dioxide during the fermentation process.

Earthy: Wine with soil-derived flavour/characteristics; mineral, damp leaves, mushrooms etc.

Easy: Undemanding, simply-flavoured.

Elegant: Stylish and refined.

Esters: Scents generated by alcohols and acids in wine. A wine is 'estery' when these characteristics are prominent.

Extract: An indication of the 'substance' of a wine, generally expressed as total extract (which would include the sugars). 18 g/l would be low, light; above 23 g/l in whites is significant; a heavy red is above 30 g/l. What wine would be without the water.

Elemental sulphur: A chemical used to dust vineyards as a control for powdery mildew.

Fermentation: The conversion of sugar to alcohol and carbon dioxide by yeast. Many of the flavours of wine are created during this process.

Filtration: Passage of wine through cellulose pads, diatomaceous earth or membranes to remove suspended solids, yeast or malolactic bacteria. Sweet wines must be filtered to remove yeast and prevent re-fermentation in the bottle.

Fining: The traditional method of clarifying wine. Insoluble substances bind with wine components and precipitate out of the liquid to reduce tannin or remove unstable proteins.

Finish: The residual sensations – tastes and textures – after swallowing. Should be pleasant (crisp, lively) and lasting in a good wine.

Finesse: Descriptor for a polished, balanced wine.

Firm: Compact, has good backbone.

Flabby: Usually means lacking in backbone, especially acid structure.

Fleshy: Very positive, meaning a wine is well fleshed out with firm texture and flavours.

Flowery: Scents and tastes with a floral aspect, as opposed to fruity (i.e. smell/taste of papaya, cantaloupe, gooseberry).

Forward: Opposite of a shy wine, with pronounced flavours and scents.

Free run: After grapes have been de-stalked and crushed, juice runs freely (without pressing). This juice is the cleanest and believed to be the most flavourful.

Fresh: Lively, youthful. Closely related to the amount of acid in the wine: a sweet wine without a backbone of acidity will cloy; enough acid and the taste is fresh and uncloying.

Full: High in alcohol and extract.

Glycerol: Product of alcoholic fermentation. Has an apparent sweetening effect on even dry wines and also gives them a slightly oily, mouth-filling character.

Green: Usually unripe, tannic and hard; sometimes simply too young.

Grip: Firm on palate and in finish. Acid, tannin, alcohol are contributors. Often not a positive term.

Graft: To splice a varietal vine to the rootstock of another type, usually one resistant to particular pests or diseases.

Gravity-flow: Winemakers prefer to rely on the natural force of gravity in the winemaking process to avoid the use of pumping. For example, in the process of racking, the undesirable solids in the wine (lees) fall to the bottom of the tank by force of gravity. The clear wine is siphoned off the lees into an empty container.

Herbaceous: Grassy, hay-like, heathery, can also indicate under-ripeness.

Hollow: Lacking substance/flavours.

Honey or honeyed: Sometimes a honey/beeswax taste or flavour; or a sign of developing maturity in some varieties, or a sign of bottle age.

Hot: Burning sensation of alcohol in finish.

Inoculation: The introduction of a special yeast culture, or any other organism, into the pressed grape juice.

Intensity: No flab, good flavour and strong character.

Lean: Thin, lacking good fruit flavours.

Lees: Sediment that occurs during winemaking or bottle ageing. Adds flavour and complexity to wines if left 'sur lie'.

Light: Wines under 10 per cent alcohol, also wines light in body (and usually short on taste).

Lively: Wines with fresh, expressive flavours.

Loam: A soil containing a mixture of clay, silt and sand that is best for the growth of most plants. Loam is not necessarily ideal for viticulture, as it can encourage excessive growth.

Long or length: Enduring; the wine's flavours linger on the palate long after swallowing.

Meaty: Suggesting a general savouriness; but also literally the aroma of meat: raw, smoked etc. Often applied to Merlot and Shiraz.

Maceration: Prolonged skin and juice contact to extract flavours, colour, and tannin, both before and after fermentation.

Malolactic fermentation: The bacterial conversion of the crisper, apple-type malic acid to the softer, milk-type lactic acid in wine. Also called ML or secondary fermentation, this conversion yields wines with greater complexity and softer acidity.

Méthode champenoise: Classic method of making champagne by inducing secondary fermentation in the bottle and producing fine bubbles. Because of French law, Cape sparkling wines made in this way are called Méthode Cap Classique (MCC).

Mouthfeel: The in-mouth impressions of wine when wine tasting, especially the tactile sensations such as 'heat' from high alcohol content or 'heaviness' or 'body' due to the viscosity from high alcohol and residual sugar in the wine.

Mousse: See bead.

Must: The skins, seeds and juice of crushed berries; may also contain whole berries or whole clusters. Red wines are fermented as must; white wines are pressed and fermented as juice.

Native yeast: Yeast occurring naturally in the winery. Cultured yeasts are generally used in winemaking.

Neutral: A wine that has a non-expressive character.

New World: Implies accessible, bold, often full-flavoured (in terms of fruit and wooding). Old World embraces terms like subtle, complex, less oaky, more varied and generally more vinous (than fruity).

Oaky: Displaying exaggerated oak/wood aromas and flavours (vanilla, spice, char, woodsmoke etc). Young wines can still outgrow oakiness, older ones do so less readily.

Oak chips: Chips of wood placed in used barrels or stainless steel tanks, used increasingly, as are oak staves to impart wood flavours. Frowned on by purists, the 'additives' approximate flavours of a new barrel and are far cheaper.

Oenologist: One who studies wine and winemaking.

Oenology: The study of wine and winemaking.

Oxidation: Change (usually for the worse) due to exposure to air, in whites often producing dark yellow or yellowish colour (called maderisation). Controlled aeration is used to introduce acceptable and desirable development in wine.

pH: A chemical notation, used in winemaking and evaluation. The pH of a wine is its effective, active acidity – not in volume but by strength or degree. The reading provides a guide to a wine's keepability. The optimum pH for a wine to age is somewhere between 3.1 and 3.4.

Palate: A term for the flavour, taste and texture of a wine.

Perfumed/scented: Strongly fragrant, can be fruity, flowery, animal etc.

Porty: Heavy, overripe, stewed; bad in an unfortified wine.

Phenolics: A large group of compounds found in grapes and wine, including many colour, tannin and flavour compounds.

Phylloxera: A tiny louse that attacks the root system of wine grape vines, responsible for killing over three million acres of vines in Europe in the 1800s. It arrived in South Africa at the turn of the century. Grafting to resistant rootstock is the only known way to combat this pest.

Pomace: The debris from grape processing which consists of stems, seeds, pulp and dead yeast cells. It can be distilled into brandy or grappa and is also called press cake.

Post-fermentation maceration: Skin contact with red wines following fermentation. Also called 'extended skin contact', the process extracts flavour compounds, colour and tannin, resulting in greater varietal character and more developed tannins.

Powdery mildew: One of several fungi that can cause severe damage to grape crops; also called oidium.

Pruning: Cutting back the vegetative part of the vine after it has become dormant. Pruning affects the size and quality of the next year's crop.

Pump-overs: The pumping of fermenting red wine over the cap of skins to extract more flavour, colour and tannin from the skins.

Racking: The gravity-siphoning or gentle pumping of the clear wine or juice off the lees for clarifying. Often used as a gentler alternative to filtration, and to aid in the wine's barrel development.

Reductive: Wine in an unevolved, unoxidised state is said to be 'reductive'; usually with a tight, sometimes unyielding character. Reductive methods: inert gas to cloak grape must is used, especially in white wine making, to inhibit oxidation.

Remontage: The process of circulating the liquid in the fermentation tank during red wine fermentation. This aerates the wine, prevents drying on the top (the cap), and encourages extraction of colour and tannins into the wine.

Rich: Flavourful, intense, generous.

Robust: Big and full bodied (but need not mean aggressive).

Rootstock: The root system of the grapevine to which a fruiting vine of any desired variety, such as Merlot, Cabernet Sauvignon, etc can be grafted.

Rough: An aggressive wine, not smooth.

Round: Well balanced, no rough edges.

Second crop: Fruit that matures after the first crop has been picked; the clusters are usually smaller and the shoots weaker. 'Na-oes' in Afrikaans.

Sharp: Describes acidity, usually unbalanced. Sometimes sharpish, fresh wine is a good food match, however.

Shoot: The current season's stem growth that bears leaves and buds.

Short or quick: Insubstantial wine, leaving the palate quickly.

Simple: One-dimensional with few flavours.

Skin contact: In winemaking, leaving the grape skins in contact with the juice or wine for a period of time, and used to extract flavour and colour from grape skins into the grape juice or wine.

Stable: When wine is in a state in which it will not develop negative characteristics in the bottle, like re-fermentation, premature browning or protein haze.

Stalky: Unripe, bitter, stemmy. Taste like green wood.

Stewed: Overripe, cooked flavours and scents. Generally not good.

Structure: Term referring to the wine's components (acid, tannin, alcohol) in relation to its ageing ability; if a wine is deemed to have 'the structure to age' it suggests these principal preservatives are in place and the wine is in balance.

Sulphites: Sulphur-based compounds used to protect wine from oxidation and bacterial activity.

Sulphur dioxide: Traditionally used to protect wine from oxidation and microbial activity during ageing.

Supple: Desirable yielding, refined texture and flavours.

Sur lie: Means 'ageing on the lees', and often referred to as 'yeast contact'. Wine is aged in the barrel with the yeast retained, rather than being clarified before ageing. Ageing on the lees increases the complexity and creaminess of the wine.

Tannins: The group of astringent and bitter compounds found in the seeds and skins of grapes which slow oxidation and promote ageing (preservative). Can be harsh and aggressive in a young wine, easing with age. Wooded wines will have wood tannins too.

Tartrate crystals: Tartaric acid, the primary acid in grapes, forms tiny crystals when chilled. These crystals adhere to the cork or form sediment in the bottle, are harmless and not considered a defect.

Terpenes: Strong, floral compounds influencing the aromas especially of Riesling, Gewürztraminer and the Muscats; with bottle-age, terpenes often develop a pungent resinous oiliness.

Terroir: Describes all the influences on the flavours in the wine that come from where the vines grow, especially soil, climate, slope, the aspect of the slope. There is no exact translation in English, but terroir is an important concept in the expression of the origin of wine.

Toasting: Heating the inside of a barrel during its construction to caramelise the flavours. This influences the flavour and aromatic characteristics of the wine during barrel ageing. Barrels can be lightly or heavily toasted.

Toasty: When barrel-fermented and aged wines show a pleasant biscuity, charry character.

Topping: During barrel ageing, some water and alcohol evaporate, concentrating the wine slightly and creating an airspace in the barrel. To prevent the harmful effects of oxygen contact with the wine, the barrel is topped-up periodically with the same wine from another container.

Trellis: The wires and stakes that support the vine.

Unfiltered: Wine that has not gone through a filtering process to clarify it.

Varietal character: The character typical of a specific grape variety.

Vegetal: Grassy, leafy, herby – in contrast to fruity, flowery, oaky.

Veraison: The stage when grapes begin to soften and gain colour.

Volatile acid (VA): That part of the acidity which can become volatile. A high reading indicates a wine prone to spoilage.

Recognised at high levels by a sharp, 'hot', vinegary smell. In South Africa, most wines must by law be below 1.2 g/l of VA; in practice, the majority are well below 1 g/l.

Viticulture: The study of grape growing.

Yeasts: Micro-organisms that secrete enzymes which convert or ferment sugar into alcohol, carbon dioxide and lesser products.

Yeast autolysis: The breakdown of yeast during ageing on the lees, a process in which chemical compounds are released that heighten the sensory qualities of the wine and increase its complexity.

Yeasty: Warm bread or baked goods smells that are often prevalent in barrel-fermented white wines and méthode champenoise sparkling wines where yeasts stay in contact with the wine after fermentation (sur lie).

GENERAL INFORMATION

Great Wine Shops

A well-stocked wine shop, where the staff are knowledgeable, is a real boon. These are the Cape's best, and they can also arrange delivery around the world.

Caroline's Fine Wines in the city centre at 15 Long Street, or at the V&A Waterfront (021) 419-8984

La Cotte Inn, Franschhoek, who also have wonderful cheeses (021) 876-3036

Vaughan Johnson's Wine & Cigar Shop at the V&A Waterfront (021) 419-2121

The Vineyard Connection, Delvera. Corner R44 and Muldersvlei Road (021) 884-4360

Wijnhuis in Stellenbosch, cnr Church and Andringa Streets (021) 887-8078

Wine Concepts in Newlands (Kildare Road) and the city (Kloof Street Lifestyle Centre) (021) 426-4401

Wine Village, Hermanus. Corner R43 & R320 (028) 316-3988

Tourism Offices

Good places to get all your general information and contacts. Brochures will also list many further activities and events.

- Cape Town central: Church Street (021) 418-5205
- V&A Waterfront: Clock Tower Precinct (021) 405-4500
- Stellenbosch: Market Street (021) 883-3584
- Paarl: Main Road (021) 872-3829
- Franschhoek: Huguenot Road (021)876-3603
- Hermanus: Main Street (028) 312-2629
- Breede River Valley (interior): Kleinplasie, Worcester (023) 347-6411

DIRECTORY
OF WINERIES

Altydgedacht: Tygerbergvalley Road (021) 976-1295.
Mon-Fri 9am-5pm, Sat 9am-1pm.
www.altydgedacht.co.za

Beaumont Wines: Main Road, Bot River, off R43 (028) 284-9450.
Mon-Fri 9.30am-12.30pm & 1.30pm-4.30pm, Sat by appointment.
www.beaumont.co.za

Boekenhoutskloof Winery: Excelsior Road, Franschhoek (021) 876-3320.
Visits by appointment.

Boschendal Wines: R310 on the Franschhoek side (021) 870-4211.
Mon-Sat May-Oct 8.30am-4.30pm, Mon-Sun Nov-Apr 8.30am-4.30pm.
www.boschendal.com

Bouchard Finlayson: Hemel en Aarde Road (R320, off R43), Hermanus (028) 312-3515.
Mon-Fri 9am-5pm, Sat 9.30am-12.30pm.
www.bouchardfinlayson.co.za

Buitenverwachting: Off M42 (Spaanschemat River Road), Constantia (021) 794-5190.
Mon-Fri 9am-5pm, Sat 9am-1pm.
www.buitenverwachting.com

Cabrière: Berg Street, Franschhoek (021) 876-2630.
Sat 11am, by appointment on weekdays and for groups.
www.cabriere.co.za

Cederberg Private Cellar: Dwarsrivier Farm. Algeria Road off the N7 to Clanwilliam (027) 482-2827.
Mon-Sat 8am-12.30 & 2pm-5pm.
www.cederbergcellars.com

Cordoba: Off R44 between Somerset West and Stellenbosch (021) 855-3744.
Sales Mon-Fri 8.30am-5pm, tastings by appointment.
www.cordobawines.co.za

Delheim: Knorhoek Road, off R44 (021) 888-4600.
Mon-Fri 9am-5pm, Sat 9am-3.30pm, Sun (Oct–Apr) 10.30am-3.30pm. Cellar tours: Mon-Fri 10.30am & 2.30pm, Sat 10.30am.
www.delheim.com

De Trafford: Mont Fleur, end (note, *the* end) of the Blaauwklippen Road, Stellenbosch (021) 880-1611.
Fri and Sat 10am-1pm only.
www.detrafford.co.za

Dornier: Blaauwklippen Road, Stellenbosch (021) 880-0557.
Mon-Fri 9am-4.30pm, Sat 9am-2pm.
www.dornierwines.co.za

Durbanville Hills: Tygerbergvalley Road (M13) (021) 558-1300.
Mon-Fri 9am-4.30pm, Sat 9.30am-2.30pm, Sun 11am-3pm.
www.durbanvillehills.co.za

Du Toitskloof Winery: R101, Rawsonville (023) 349-1601.
Cellar: Mon-Fri 8am-5pm, Sat 9am-12.30pm. Shop: Mon-Sat
8am-5pm, Sun 11am-4pm.
www.dutoitskloof.com

Eikendal: R44, Stellenbosch (021) 855-1422.
Oct-Apr Mon-Fri 9.30am-4.30pm, Sat/Sun 10.30am-3pm. May-
Sept Mon-Fri 10.30am-3pm, Sat/Sun 10am-1pm.
www.eikendal.com

Fairview: Suid-Agter Paarl Road, Paarl (021) 863-2450.
Mon-Fri 8.30am-5pm, Sat 8.30am-1pm.
www.fairview.co.za

Flagstone Winery: Heartland AECI, De Beers Road, Somerset
West (021) 686-8640.
Tues-Sat 10am-6pm.
www.flagstonewines.com

Fleur du Cap: Cnr Adam Tas & Plankenbrug Road, Stellenbosch
(021) 809-8492.
Mon-Fri 8am-5pm, Sat 10am-1pm.
www.fleurducap.co.za

Fort Simon: Fischers Road off Bottelary Road, Kuilsriver (021)
903-8034.
Mon-Fri 9.30am-5pm, Sat 10am-2pm.
www.fortsimon.co.za

Glen Carlou: Simondium Road, off R44, Paarl (021) 875-5528.
Mon-Fri 8.45am-4.45pm, Sat 9am-12.30pm.
www.glencarlou.co.za

Graham Beck Wines: *Robertson*: R60 between Robertson and
Worcester (023) 626-1214.
Mon-Fri 9am-5pm, Sat 10am-3pm.
Coastal: R45 outside Franschhoek (021) 874-1258.
Mon-Fri 9am-5pm, Sat 10am-3pm.
www.grahambeckwines.co.za

Grangehurst: Eikendal Road, off R44 (021) 855-3625.
Mon-Fri 9am-4pm.
www.grangehurst.co.za

Groot Constantia Estate: Constantia Road, Constantia (021) 794-
5128.
Mon-Sun 9am-6pm (5pm May-Nov).
www.grootconstantia.co.za

Groote Post: Darling Hills Road off R27 West Coast Road (022)
492-2825.
Mon-Fri 9am-5pm, Sat 9am-3pm.
www.grootepost.com

Hamilton Russell Vineyards: Hemel en Aarde Road (R320, off
R43), Hermanus (028) 312-3595.
Mon-Fri 9am-5pm, Sat 9am-1pm.
www.hamiltonrussellvineyards.co.za

Hartenberg Estate: M23 Bottelary Road, Koelenhof (021) 865-
2541.
Mon-Fri 9am-5pm, Sat 9am-3pm.
www.hartenbergestate.com

Hazendal: Bottelary Road M23 (021) 903-5112.
Mon-Fri 8.30am-4.30, Sat-Sun 10am-3pm.
www.hazendal.co.za

Jordan Wine Estate: Stellenbosch Kloof Road, Vlottenberg (021) 881-3441.
Mon-Fri (Nov-April) 10am-4.30pm, Sat 9.30am-2.30pm. Sat closes 12.30pm other months.
www.jordanwines.com

Kanonkop Estate: R44 between Stellenbosch and Klapmuts (021) 884-4656.
Mon-Fri 8.30am-5pm, Sat 9am-12.30pm. Tours by appointment.
www.kanonkop.co.za

Klein Constantia Estate: Klein Constantia Road (021) 794-5188.
Mon-Fri 9am-5pm, Sat 9am-1pm.
www.kleinconstantia.com

KWV: 57 Main Street, Paarl (021) 807-3008.
Tours Mon-Sat 10am, 10.30am, 14.15 pm and 10.15am (in German).
www.kwv-international.com

La Petite Ferme: Pass Road, Franschhoek (021) 876-3016.
Mon-Sun 12pm-4pm.
www.lapetiteferme.co.za

Meerlust: On R310 (off N2 to Stellenbosch) (021) 843-3587.
Sales: Mon-Thurs 9am-5pm, Fri 9am-4.30pm.
www.meerlust.co.za

Meinert: Winery not open to public, tastings at 96 Winery Road Restaurant, Winery Road off R44 (021) 842-2020.
www.meinert.co.za

Môreson: Happy Valley Road, Franschhoek (021) 876-3055.
Mon-Sun 11am-5pm.
www.moreson.co.za

Morgenhof: Klapmuts Road (R44) (021) 889-5510.
Nov-Apr: Mon-Fri 9am-5.30pm, Sat-Sun 10am-5pm. May-Oct: Mon-Fri 9am-4.30pm, Sat-Sun 10am-3pm.
www.morgenhof.com

Morgenster Estate: Lourensford Road, Somerset West (021) 852-1738.
Mon-Fri 10am-5pm.
www.morgenster.co.za

Muratie: Knorhoek Road, off R44, Stellenbosch (021) 865-2330.
Mon-Fri 9am-5pm, Sat-Sun 10am-4pm.
www.muratie.co.za

Nederburg Wines: Sonstraal Road, Daljosafat, Paarl (021) 877-5132.
Mon-Fri 8.30am-5pm, Sat 10am-2pm, Nov-Mar also Sun 10am-4pm.
www.nederburg.co.za

Neethlingshof: M12 Road between Stellenbosch and Kuilsriver (021) 883-8988.
Mon-Fri 9am-5pm, Sat-Sun 10am-4pm.
www.neethlingshof.co.za

Neil Ellis: Jonkershoek Road, Stellenbosch (021) 887-0649.
Mon-Fri 9.30am-4.30pm, Sat 10am-2pm.
www.neilellis.co.za

Paul Cluver Estate: De Rust Estate, Elgin. Turn left at Kromco on
the N2 (021) 844-0605.
Mon-Fri 8:30am-5pm, Sat 9am-2pm.
www.cluver.com

Plaisir de Merle: R45 between Paarl and Franschhoek (021) 874-
1071.
Mon-Fri 8.30am-5pm, Sat Nov-Mar 10am-4pm, Apr-Oct 10am-
2pm.
www.plaisirdemerle.co.za

Rustenberg Wines: Rustenberg Road, Stellenbosch (021) 809-
1200.
Mon-Fri 9am-4.30pm, Sat 10am-1.30pm (3.30pm in Dec/Jan).
www.rustenberg.co.za

Rust en Vrede Estate: Annandale Road, Stellenbosch (021) 881-
3881.
Mon-Fri 9am-5pm, Sat 9am-4pm (3pm in winter).
www.rustenvrede.com

Sadie Family Wines: Aprilskloof Road, Paardeberg (021) 869-
8349.
Visits strictly by appointment only.

Saxenberg: Polkadraai Road, between Kuilsriver and Stellenbosch
(021) 903-6113.
Mon-Fri 9am-5pm, Sat 10am-4pm, Sun (Sep-May) 10am-4pm.
www.saxenberg.co.za

Simonsig Wine Estate: Kromme Rhee Road, Koelenhof, between R44 & R304 (021) 888-4900.
Mon-Fri 8.30am-5pm, Sat 8.30am-4pm.
www.simonsig.co.za

Spier: Annandale Road, Stellenbosch (021) 809-1143.
Mon-Sun 9am-5pm.
www.spier.co.za

Springfield Estate: R317 (Bonnievale Road), just outside Robertson (023) 626-3661.
Mon-Fri 8am-5pm, Sat 9am-4pm.
www.springfieldestate.com

Stellenbosch Hills: Corner R310 and Old Vlottenburg Road (021) 881-3828.
Mon-Fri 9am-4.45pm, Sat 9am-12.15pm.
www.stellenboschhills.co.za (under construction)

Stellenbosch Vineyards: *Welmoed Winery*: R310 Stellenbosch (021) 881-3870.
Mon-Sat 9am-5pm, Sun 10am-4pm.
Helderberg Winery: Winery Road, off R44 (021) 842-2012.
Mon-Fri 9am-5.30pm, Sat 9am-5pm.
www.stellvine.co.za

Stellenzicht: Stellenrust Road, off Blaauwklippen Road, Stellenbosch (021) 880-1103.
Mon-Fri 9am-5pm, Sat-Sun 10am-4pm.
www.stellenzicht.co.za

Thelema Mountain Vineyards: R310 Helshoogte Pass (021) 885-1924.

Mon-Fri 9am-5pm, Sat 9am-1pm.
www.thelema.co.za

Tokara: Helshoogte Pass (021) 808-5900.
Mon-Fri 10am-5pm. Tours by appointment.
www.tokara.co.za

Uitkyk: R44 between Stellenbosch and Paarl (021) 884-4416.
Mon-Fri 9am-5pm, Sat-Sun 10am-4pm.
www.uitkyk.co.za

Van Loveren Private Cellar: R317 between Robertson and
Bonnievale (023) 615-1505.
Mon-Fri 8.30am-5pm, Sat 9.30am-1pm.
www.vanloveren.co.za

Vergelegen: Lourensford Road, Somerset West (021) 874-1334.
9.30am-4.30pm daily, guided cellar tours daily.
www.vergelegen.co.za

Vergenoegd: R310 to Stellenbosch shortly after turning off N2
(021) 843-3248.
Mon-Fri 8am-4pm, Sat 9.30am-12.30pm.
www.vergenoegd.co.za

Villiera Wines: R304 at Koelenhof interchange (exit 39 off N1)
(021) 865-2002.
Mon-Fri 8.30am-5pm, Sat 8.30am-1pm.
www.villiera.com

Warwick Estate: R44 between Klapmuts and Stellenbosch (021)
884-3146.
Mon-Fri 10am-5pm, Sat 10am-4pm, Sun (Oct-Apr) 10am-4pm.
www.warwickwine.co.za

Waterford Estate: Blaauwklippen Road, off R44, Stellenbosch
(021) 880-0496.
Mon-Fri 9am-5pm, Sat 10am-1pm.
www.waterfordwines.com

Zorgvliet: Helshoogte Pass (021) 885-1399.
Mon-Thurs 9am-5pm, Fri to 6pm, Sat 10am-7pm, Sun 10am-
5pm. Visiting times may be more limited in winter.
www.zorgvlietwines.co.za

> *'When round the festive board we sit*
> *And pass around the wine,*
> *Remember though abuse is vile,*
> *Yet use can be divine.*
> *'Twas heaven in kindness sent the grape*
> *To please both great and small,*
> *'Tis little fools who drink too much*
> *And big fools not at all.'*

Dr Samuel Johnson

INDEX